The Brief English Workbook
Second Edition

To Accompany

The Brief English Handbook
Fifth Edition

Edward A. Dornan
Charles W. Dawe
Orange Coast College

HarperCollins*CollegePublishers*

The Brief English Workbook, Second Edition, To Accompany the Brief English Handbook, Fifth Edition
by Edward A. Dornan and Charles W. Dawe

ISBN: 0-673-52515-5
96 97 98 99 00 9 8 7 6 5 4 3 2 1

Contents

Sentence Clarity and Variety 75

Punctuation 93

Mechanics 129

Preface

The Brief English Workbook is a practice book in the elements of writing with exercises through which students can test their understanding and mastery of basic writing principles.

The organization of The Brief English Workbook parallels that of chapters 1-14 and 16-39 of The Brief English Handbook by the same authors. The workbook can be used as a supplement for those teachers who want additional exercises for their students.

The first part, "Grammar," presents exercises on parts of speech, parts of sentences, phrase and clauses.

In the second part, "Sentence Errors," exercises cover common mistakes writers make when expressing their thoughts in writing—fragments, comma splices and fused sentences, failure to establish the correct relations between subjects and verbs as well as between pronouns and antecedents—the kind of errors that hinder clear communication.

The third part, "Sentence Clarity and Variety," continues the work with sentences, emphasizing ways to write clear and accurate sentences while keeping a reader interested. Some of the techniques the exercises ask students to practice are varying sentence patterns, using modifiers, arranging words for emphasis, organizing sentences through subordination and coordination, and enhancing the impact of sentences through parallel structure.

In the fourth and fifth parts, "Punctuation" and "Mechanics," exercises cover using commas, semicolons, colons, dashes, capitalization, abbreviations, and the like.

We have tried to make these practices and exercises lively and interesting; whenever possible, they present a common theme or topic rather than a series of unrelated sentences.

Answers to the exercises are included in the text so that students can use this workbook as a self-study text.

We wish to thank Ellen Schatz, Basic Skills Acquisitions Editor, and Mark Gerrard, Supplements Editor of HarperCollins for their valuable aid in the production of this book.

EAD

CWD

EXERCISE 1: IDENTIFYING NOUNS AND PRONOUNS

Underline the nouns and circle the pronouns in the following sentences. Write the number of nouns and pronouns you find in the space provided after each sentence.

EXAMPLE

Several <u>centuries</u> ago in <u>Japan</u>, <u>ninjas</u> were <u>spies</u> and <u>assassins</u>.

Nouns _____*5*_____ Pronouns _____*0*_____

1. They were considered to be elite servants of the government.

Nouns _____ Pronouns _____

2. Ninjas dressed in a coarse black uniform and wore a black scarf wrapped around their heads, revealing only their eyes.

Nouns _____ Pronouns _____

3. They could move undetected through the night, often appearing out of shadows to attack an enemy.

Nouns _____ Pronouns _____

4. Ninjas were trained in hand-to-hand combat called ninjutsu.

Nouns _____ Pronouns _____

5. With one blow, a ninja could kill an opponent.

Nouns _____ Pronouns _____

6. These warriors were also trained in the use of weapons, such as throwing stars and samurai swords.

Nouns _____ Pronouns _____

7. Some ninjas could split an attacker in half because they were so deadly with a sword.

Nouns _____ Pronouns _____

8. Ancient ninjas also trained in mystical practices that would help them attain spiritual enlightenment.

   Nouns _____ Pronouns _____

9. When not in the service of the government, they retreated to the mountains of central Japan to seek mystical fulfillment.

   Nouns _____ Pronouns _____

10. By practicing martial arts and mysticism, ninjas became known as warriors who were in harmony with nature and civilization.

    Nouns _____ Pronouns _____

11. Today, the image of these ancient warriors is troubling.

    Nouns _____ Pronouns _____

12. The ninja is glamorized in books and karate movies, becoming a superhero for the young, in much the same way that Superman was for their parents.

    Nouns _____ Pronouns _____

13. But unlike the caped crusader, the modern-day ninja poses problems for the police.

    Nouns _____ Pronouns _____

14. Recently, a fourteen-year-old boy dressed like a ninja threatened an officer with nunchakus, which are two oak sticks connected with a chain and used to whip or strangle a victim.

    Nouns _____ Pronouns _____

15. Police discovered the boy was part of a gang that dressed in black uniforms and extorted money from other children.

    Nouns _____ Pronouns _____

16. In another incident police shot a man dressed like a ninja who attacked two officers with a sword.

    Nouns _____ Pronouns _____

17. Psychologists report that the behavior of those who dress and act the part of ninjas has become commonplace.

    Nouns _____ Pronouns _____

18. People emulate characters like ninjas to help them find their own identity, but this does not mean they are potential criminals.

    Nouns _____ Pronouns _____

19. Still, the number of attacks made by ninjas is rising.

    Nouns _____ Pronouns _____

20. The ninja today has been created by mass media and seems distant from the historic ninja, who served his government and searched for enlightenment.

    Nouns _____ Pronouns _____

EXERCISE 2: IDENTIFYING VERBS

In the following sentences underline the verbs and verb phrases and label them as transitive (T), intransitive (I), linking (L), or helping (H).

EXAMPLE

Many uninitiated Americans (view) computer experts as sorcerers.

1. To these Americans, computer knowledge is a secret art.

2. This view seems true because of the mysterious actions of young computer hackers.

3. Hackers dedicate their lives to an exploration of computer power.

4. Often this exploration has dramatic results.

5. Recently a group of New Jersey teenage hackers pooled their knowledge and machinery.

6. By telephone they entered the data banks of a dozen computers across the country.

7. At first they gleaned only private information.

8. For instance, they acquired secret Pentagon telephone numbers.

9. They also collected credit card numbers.

10. Soon after that, they made fraudulent computer purchases.

11. With the credit card numbers, they unlawfully accumulated $30,000 in computer equipment.

12. One of their alleged feats is almost unbelievable.

13. These teen-age hackers may have changed a satellite orbit.

14. Authorities, however, deny this claim.

15. Is their claim true? Did the New Jersey hackers shift a satellite in space?

16. No one knows. But, in any case, creative hackers are becoming major problems for authorities.

17. Last year alone, U.S. businesses spent $600 million on computer security equipment.

18. By the next decade, computer security costs could exceed $2 billion.

19. Who will pay the bill?

20. No doubt the cost of goods and services will rise.

EXERCISE 3: IDENTIFYING ADJECTIVES AND ADVERBS

Each of the following sentences contains at least one adjective or adverb. Some sentences contain both. In the following sentences underline the adjectives and adverbs and label them ADJ or ADV. Do not mark the articles *the, a,* or *an.*

EXAMPLE   *ADJ*   *ADJ*   *ADJ ADJ*
Although <u>alligator</u> hunting is <u>illegal</u> in Florida, the state has licensed <u>several</u> <u>alligator</u> trappers.

1. Mike Fagan, potbellied and tan with a nimble smile, is one of those trappers.

2. Fagan traps nuisance alligators that have become highly dangerous.

3. He expresses deep appreciation and cautious respect for alligators.

4. He claims they keep the rodent and snake populations down but can outrun a dog and crush and swallow it as quickly as you can wink.

5. Alligators are almost always afraid of humans.

6. Unfortunately, they sometimes do attack people.

7. A mother alligator will always attack when a human blocks her from her nest.

8. A bull alligator will attack if a human swims nearby.

9. All alligators will attack if humans feed them until they associate humans with supper.

10. Fagan traps nuisance alligators in two ways.

11. He hangs a shark hook on a cypress branch near a pond and baits the hook with a very large piece of beef lung, smelly as old garbage.

12. Next, he splashes some beef blood into the creek, sending the pungent odor everywhere with the ripples, and waits.

13. Fagan claims a trapper must be very patient because a bull might sit under the hook for three days.

14. Although the beast has a brain the size of a thumbnail, he is fairly smart, knowing that the meat has not appeared before.

15. Eventually, the alligator takes the meat in his mouth, quickly rears his head, and swallows, finally hooked.

16. Nightly in the summer, Fagan traps alligators from a flat-bottom boat.

17. He scans the water for a pair of eyes that glow like hot coals.

18. Fagan fires a barbed dart into the soft flesh of the jaws.

19. The alligator fights, but the alligator always loses the battle.

20. Fagan sells the lumpy hide to tanners and the white meat to Miami restaurants.

EXERCISE 4: IDENTIFYING PREPOSITIONS, CONJUNCTIONS, AND INTERJECTIONS

Underline the prepositions and circle the conjunctions and interjections in the following sentences. Write the numbers of prepositions, conjunctions, and interjections in the spaces provided after each sentence.

EXAMPLE

<u>In</u> the past, historical studies was an important activity <u>for</u> students(and)scholars.

Prepositions ____2____ Conjunctions ____1____ Interjections ____0____

1. Now students often are not interested in the study of history, proclaiming, "Oh no! It

   doesn't relate to me."

   Prepositions _____ Conjunctions _____ Interjections _____

2. The response is not a matter of ignorance but of real concern that history seldom relates to

   ordinary people, especially to women and children, who comprise three-fourths of

   humankind.

   Prepositions _____ Conjunctions _____ Interjections _____

3. A few members of the ruling classes appear in history books, but learning about the bottom
   90 percent of the population was virtually impossible until modern times.

   Prepositions _____ Conjunctions _____ Interjections _____

4. This lack of knowledge comes not only from ignorance but also from the distortion of his-

   torical sources.

   Prepositions _____ Conjunctions _____ Interjections _____

5. Most knowledge about ancient and medieval heresies and witchcraft comes from religious

   leaders opposed to nonconformist behavior.

   Prepositions _____ Conjunctions _____ Interjections _____

6. Most surviving accounts of slave revolts in antiquity and of peasant revolts in the Middle Ages come from men opposed to rebellious causes.

   Prepositions _____   Conjunctions _____   Interjections _____

7. Only recently has the official history of native Americans been revised, for the original version was written by government officials, missionaries, and frontiersmen.

   Prepositions _____   Conjunctions _____   Interjections _____

8. Now we feel the pull and tug of historical biases when we read official accounts of the Vietnam War and of the political scandal called "Watergate."

   Prepositions _____   Conjunctions _____   Interjections _____

9. Students seem comfortable in the mainstream of hard facts but uncomfortable in the murky backwaters of historical interpretation.

   Prepositions _____   Conjunctions _____   Interjections _____

10. How sad! Those who ignore history may be condemned to repeat it.

   Prepositions _____   Conjunctions _____   Interjections _____

EXERCISE 5: IDENTIFYING SUBJECTS AND PREDICATES

Underline the complete subject and circle the simple subject in each of the following sentences.

EXAMPLE

Several shark (attacks) have taken place off the coast of northern California.

1. Abalone divers and surfers are the most frequent victims of shark attacks.

2. Paul Parsons, a skin diver, was mauled north of San Francisco.

3. Tricia Kim, a surfer, watched a twelve-foot shark clamp down on the front of her surfboard.

4. Authorities have been stunned by the number of attacks in such quick succession.

5. Sharks attacked a total of three people in the Pacific between 1951 and 1955.

6. That number has quadrupled during the last four years.

7. The center of the danger area runs from Monterey Bay to Point Reyes, California.

8. This ninety-mile stretch of coast and the Farallon islands to the west form a wedge called the Red Triangle.

9. It may be the shark-attack capital of the world.

10. The assailants in every case are huge great whites.

Underline the complete predicate and circle the simple predicate in each of the following sentences. Remember, a simple predicate may include helping verbs.

EXAMPLE

A great white shark (was) the villain of the popular film *Jaws.*

11. Many biologists trace the shark attacks to recent animal protection rulings.

12. New laws make it illegal to hunt seals and otters.

13. These sea creatures are staples in the great white's diet.

14. Fifteen elephant seals lived and bred in the Red Triangle in 1961.

15. Over five thousand elephant seals flourished there just last year.

16. The sea lion population has been increasing 5 percent a year.

17. Great whites are responding to the increase in food supply by producing larger litters more rapidly.

18. Great whites normally avoid humans but can mistake a diver in a black wet suit for a seal.

19. Are great whites becoming a serious threat to California swimmers?

20. Deaths from sharks are still fewer than deaths from lightning bolts or snakebites.

EXERCISE 6: IDENTIFYING COMPLEMENTS

Underline and label the direct objects (DO), indirect objects (IO), predicate adjectives (PA), and predicate nominatives (PN) in the following sentences. Do not mark modifying words. If a sentence does not have a direct object, indirect object, predicate adjective, or predicate nominative, write *none* in the margin by its number.

EXAMPLE

$$DO \qquad\qquad\qquad\qquad\qquad\qquad\qquad\qquad\qquad\qquad DO$$

Pests and diseases destroy <u>one-third</u> of the world's crop harvests each year and threaten <u>millions</u>

of people with starvation.

1. A pest in agriculture is any organism capable of crop destruction.

2. Pests include harmful insects, mammals, birds, and diseases.

3. Pests may ravage crops at any time during growth, harvest, or storage.

4. The problem is more severe in developing countries.

5. Humankind is waging a battle with pests.

6. Chemical pesticides give farmers the edge in the battle against pests.

7. The pesticides have serious drawbacks, however.

8. Sometimes pesticides become less potent with extensive use.

9. Pesticides also kill the enemies of pests.

10. The inadvertent death of harmless creatures gives scientists a problem to solve.

11. When their natural enemies die, pest populations increase dramatically.

12. Pests then become an even greater threat to crops.

13. Pesticides also threaten the food chain.

14. Small creatures eat crops that have been sprayed with poison pesticides.

15. Larger creatures eat the smaller creatures and become poisoned.

16. In this way pesticides taint the food chain and threaten even humans.

17. The damage pesticides do to the food chain is real and has influenced the work of biological researchers.

18. This problem has alerted them to the danger of pesticides.

19. The solution is simple; the researchers must find new forms of crop protection or face the destruction of the food chain.

20. Difficult and challenging is the problem ahead of them.

EXERCISE 7: USING PREPOSITIONAL PHRASES

Use the following prepositions to write sentences that include prepositional phrases. Underline the prepositional phrase in each sentence you write. Get a daily newspaper and use news items as the topics of your sentences.

EXAMPLE

on _____ *Two people survived a plane crash on the Torrance* _____
_____ *Airport runway.* _____

1. during _____

   _____

2. in _____

   _____

3. across _____

   _____

4. of _____

   _____

5. on _____

   _____

6. under _____

   _____

7. through _____

   _____

8. behind _____

   _____

9. above _____

_____

10. around _____

_____

11. for _____

_____

12. by _____

_____

13. into _____

_____

14. between _____

_____

15. before _____

_____

16. after _____

_____

17. against _____

_____

18. at _____

_____

19. beside _____

_____

20. out _____

_____

EXERCISE 8: USING APPOSITIVES

Combine each of the following groups of sentences into one sentence by using appositives. You will have to revise wording and exclude some words to make the combined sentences read correctly. Set off appositive phrases with commas and underline them.

EXAMPLE

General Motors will open a new plant next year. General Motors is America's largest automaker.

General Motors, America's largest automaker, will open a

new plant next year.

1. *TV Guide* publishes local television listings and articles about TV celebrities and shows. *TV Guide* is the best-selling weekly magazine in the world.

   _____

   _____

   _____

2. Authorities claim that a nine-millimeter Ingram is currently America's most dangerous street weapon. The Ingram is an automatic submachine gun .

   _____

   _____

   _____

3. *2001: A Space Odyssey* is still a popular cult film. *2001: A Space Odyssey* is an early Stanley Kubrick success.

   _____

   _____

   _____

4. Scoop McLain stopped at Bernie's place last night. He was as sarcastic and swaggering as ever.

_____

_____

_____

5. Soap operas are popular TV entertainment. Soap operas involve love, betrayal, success, and failure.

_____

_____

_____

6. Millions read *Cosmopolitan*. *Cosmopolitan* is called *Cosmo* by its avid admirers.

_____

_____

_____

7. Weightlifting does very little for the cardiovascular system. Weightlifting is a popular sport among young men and women.

_____

_____

_____

8. Coca-Cola has changed its flavor to compete more effectively with Pepsi-Cola. Coca-Cola is still the largest selling soft drink.

_____

_____

_____

9. Elvis Presley's death came in 1977. His death was a shock to millions of fans.

_____

_____

_____

10. Richard Hollingshead opened the world's first drive-in theater. He was a New Jersey businessman. A drive-in theater is a massive parking lot equipped with movie screen and speakers in the stalls.

_____

_____

_____

_____

_____

EXERCISE 9: USING PREPOSITIONAL PHRASES AND APPOSITIVES

Combine each of the following groups of sentences into one sentence by using prepositional phrases and appositives. You will have to revise wording and exclude some words to make the combined sentences read correctly. Set off appositives with commas. Underline the prepositional phrases and appositives.

EXAMPLE

Jesus and Manny are my older brothers. They argued constantly. They argued during the entire trip. They sat in the back seat.

Jesus and Manny, my older brothers, argued in the back seat during the entire trip.

1. Pope John Paul II visited Mehmet Ali Agca. Agca is the man who shot the pope. The visit took place in prison.

_____

_____

_____

2. The 1957 Chevrolet is still popular. It came with large tail fins. It is popular among rare car collectors.

_____

_____

_____

3. A Beverly Hills detective was arrested. The detective is Axel Foley. He was arrested for disturbing the peace.

_____

_____

_____

4. Bill Linn predicted John F. Kennedy would be killed. Linn is a spiritual medium. He lives in New York.

_____

_____

_____

5. Belle Starr was shot to death. She was a notorious outlaw. She died in Oklahoma. She was forty-one years old.

_____

_____

_____

6. Eric Fischl portrays the anxiety he experiences. Fischl is a forty-three-year-old artist. He sees the anxiety in American life

_____

_____

_____

7. Once again the tango is becoming popular. The tango is a dance that began a century ago in Buenos Aires bordellos. It is becoming popular in New York nightspots.

_____

_____

_____

8. Logic bombs are exploding every week. Logic bombs are bits of destructive software coding designed to confuse a computer system. They are exploding in the country's leading business firms.

_____

_____

_____

9. *Time* magazine quoted John Dryden: "Forgiveness to the injured doth belong." Dryden was an English poet and critic. *Time* quoted Dryden in its May 20, 1985, issue.

_____

_____

_____

10. Mary Harris organized labor unions. She was a native of Cork, Ireland. She organized unions in West Virginia, Pennsylvania, and Colorado.

_____

_____

_____

NAME _____   DATE_____

EXERCISE 10: IDENTIFYING INFINITIVE AND PARTICIPLE PHRASES

Underline and identify the infinitive (INF) and participle (PART) phrases in the following sentences. Be sure to include all modifiers and complements that are part of the phrases.

EXAMPLE

INF

Throughout history humankind has been unable <u>to master time</u>.

1. Once, communities decreed noon to be the moment the sun reached its zenith.

2. Today, business executives, traumatized by stiff competition, watch their watches as intensely as they watch their bank balances.

3. "Time is money," claims a time-conscious broker, holding a phone receiver in each hand to place stock orders.

4. Discouraged by time's power, the Roman poet Ovid said, "Time, the devourer of all things."

5. Whether time is used to organize or to traumatize our lives, we cannot resist its unrelenting movement.

Combine the following groups of sentences by using infinitive and participle phrases. Be sure to follow the directions in brackets after each sentence. At times you will need to change the tense of some verbs, add new words, and delete words.

EXAMPLE

Time ticks away in relentless beats. It is a major preoccupation of most Americans.
[Use a present participle phrase.]

Ticking away in relentless beats, time is a major preoccupation of most Americans.

6. Our lives are paced precisely. The atomic clock is a perfect machine.
   [Use an infinitive phrase.]

   _____

   _____

   _____

7. Precise timekeeping is necessary. It aids submarine navigation, oil exploration, and television transmission. [Use an infinitive phrase.]

_____

_____

_____

8. The Navy sends a 150-pound atomic clock to other countries. The atomic clock is named Mr. *Clock*. Technicians use Mr. Clock in the adjustment of other timekeeping systems. [Use an infinitive phrase and a past participle phrase.]

_____

_____

_____

_____

9. The timekeepers at the Naval Observatory have one main duty. They must keep precise time for a system of navigation satellites. [Use an infinitive phrase.]

_____

_____

_____

10. Navigation satellites will soon monitor world time. They are positioned precisely in the sky. They permit official time to be beamed to clocks everywhere. [Use a present participial phrase and an infinitive phrase.]

_____

_____

_____

_____

In each of the following spaces, write a sentence related to the subject time that includes one or more infinitive, present participle, or past participle phrases. Underline each phrase.

EXAMPLE

Jimmy is old enough to tell the time, but young enough to be unconcerned about its passing.

11. _____

_____

_____

12. _____

_____

_____

13. _____

_____

_____

14. _____

_____

_____

15. _____

_____

_____

EXERCISE 11: USING GERUNDS AND PARTICIPLES

Write two sentences for each of the following words. In the first sentence use the word in a gerund phrase. In the second, use the word in a present participle phrase.

EXAMPLE

riding

GERUND PHRASE   *Riding a bike is fun.*

PARTICIPIAL PHRASE   *Riding on the car fender, Jill felt the wind whip her hair.*

1. camping _____

_____

_____

_____

2. fighting _____

_____

_____

_____

3. hoping _____

_____

_____

_____

4. dying _____

_____

_____

_____

5. drifting _____

_____

_____

_____

6. screaming _____

_____

_____

_____

7. flinging _____

_____

_____

_____

8. washing _____

_____

_____

_____

9. wading _____

_____

_____

_____

10. speaking _____

_____

_____

_____

EXERCISE 12: WRITING ABSOLUTE PHRASES

Combine each of the following sets of sentences using absolute phrases. To create readable sentences, you will sometimes have to leave out words, add new words, and change the tense of verbs. Continue to revise your sentences until they read smoothly.

EXAMPLE

The players were leaning over their cards. They were chatting softly. The poker game continued for hours.

The players leaning over their cards and chatting softly, the poker game continued for hours.

1. The restaurant was closed for the night. The street seemed strangely empty.

_____

_____

_____

2. The election was over. The votes remained to be counted and the winners to be announced.

_____

_____

_____

3. Tina stood on the riverbank and reeled in the trout. The rod was bending like a whip. Its tip was vibrating like a snake's tongue.

_____

_____

_____

4. The wind whipped over the roof of the abandoned house. The soft rumble was echoing through the empty room.

_____

_____

_____

5. The tile was growing wet from the steam. Ian felt the slick floor beneath his bare feet.

_____

_____

_____

EXERCISE 13: IDENTIFYING CLAUSES

In each of the following sentences, a clause is printed in italics. If the italicized clause functions as a main clause, place an M above it. If the italicized clause functions as a dependent clause, place a D above it, and if it functions as a noun clause, place an N above it.

EXAMPLE

D

Although most Americans feel safe in their own neighborhoods, they are not.

1. *Because 45 percent of all adult Americans keep at least one gun,* the risk of being shot is high.

2. In California alone, there are at least 5 million handguns, according to the Bureau of Alcohol, Tobacco, and Firearms, *which is responsible for compiling such official information.*

3. *The presence of guns increases the likelihood of fatal injuries,* and aggressive behavior makes injuries certain.

4. *That people will use guns to kill* is not a question.

5. Guns seem to be a cue for violence and also give their owners a sense of power *that may lead to overreaction.*

In the following sentences underline the dependent clauses and identify them as adjective (ADJ) or as adverb clauses (ADV). There may be more than one dependent clause in a sentence.

EXAMPLE

ADV

It is difficult to predict <u>when a person will act violently.</u>

6. People in a state of high arousal, which means full of anxiety, frustration, and stress, are more likely to act aggressively.

7. Crowding and health factors like hypoglycemia, which is a disease that affects blood sugar levels, may affect hostility.

8. Many film directors who are successful exalt violent heroes because these heroes make money at the box office.

9. But the cost, if you believe films affect behavior, can only be measured in pain and suffer-

   ing, not in dollars.

10. One authority who believes displaced aggression is increasing claims that when a solid 25

    percent of the population is capable of committing random violence, we should have a film

    rating system.

Combine each of the following groups of sentences by using dependent clauses as indicated in the instructions in brackets. You may need to change some words to avoid needless repetition.

EXAMPLE
Even more shocking is the belief that 2 to 5 percent of the population are true sociopaths. They will do anything to get their way. [Use *who* to form an adjective clause.]

Even more shocking is the belief that 2 to 5 percent of the

population are sociopaths, who will do anything to get their way.

11. Do you expect sociopaths to be ruthless killers? You are wrong. Many of them are profes-
    sionals, such as lawyers, doctors, and bankers. [Use *if* and *because* to form two adverb
    clauses.]

    _____

    _____

    _____

    _____

12. Ten percent of the population may be antisocial. They include drug abusers, juvenile delin-
    quents, and people with explosive behavior. [Use *which* to form an adjective clause.]

    _____

    _____

    _____

13. Antisocial behavior will become more common. Drug abuse and violent behavior is increasing among ten- to thirteen-year-olds. [Use *because* to form an adverb clause.]

_____

_____

_____

14. Children grow up with little parental concern or supervision. Society becomes the victim. [Use *as* to form an adverb clause.]

_____

_____

_____

15. Many people handle the threat by enrolling in self-defense classes or by arming themselves. They are the most fearful of sudden attack. [Use *who* to form an adjective clause.]

_____

_____

_____

16. Many people with explosive personality disorders realize they get in too much trouble chasing strangers home or brandishing crowbars in parking lots. They eventually confine their outbursts to their homes. [Use *after* to form an adverb clause.]

_____

_____

_____

17. Some people have built-in cultural values that might inhibit aggressive displays toward family members. Other people show aggression to family members they would not show to friends. [Use *while* to form an adverb clause.]

_____

_____

_____

18. Violence erupts outside the family. The victims are often employees of large companies or government agencies. These companies and agencies deal with the public. [Use *when* to form an adverb clause, and use *that* to form an adjective clause.]

_____

_____

_____

19. Many companies and agencies do not want to completely satisfy complaining clients. They have thousands of complaints weekly. [Use *that* to form an adjective clause.]

_____

_____

_____

20. An aggressive client becomes angry. The employee listens to the complaint. The employee becomes the target. [Use *as* to form an adverb clause and *who* to form an adjective clause.]

_____

_____

_____

EXERCISE 1: CORRECTING SENTENCE FRAGMENTS

Correct each of the following fragments, either by attaching it to a main clause or by rewriting the fragment as a complete sentence. Mark correct items with a C.

EXAMPLE

Dragons guarded buried treasure better than any other animal. Because they could see even tiny objects at great distances.

Dragons guarded buried treasure better than any other animal because they could see even tiny objects at great distances.

1. Because Chinese scholars have been so careful to record details over so many centuries. We have more interesting information about Chinese dragons than dragons of other cultures.

   _____

   _____

   _____

   _____

2. Most dragons, for example, laid their eggs near rivers. While a few preferred hillsides.

   _____

   _____

   _____

3. The hatching of a dragon egg had an impressive effect on the weather. Causing the wind to increase if the newborn were male and almost cease if it were female.

   _____

   _____

   _____

4. Terrible rainstorms, accompanied by thunder, lightning, and almost complete darkness announced a dragon's birth. "Eyewitness" accounts agree on the severity of these storms.

_____

_____

_____

_____

_____

5. Great emphasis was placed on the number of scales and claws a dragon possessed. In the dragon literature of China.

_____

_____

_____

6. Some scholars argued that a real dragon had exactly eighty-one scales. A figure obtained by squaring the masculine number nine.

_____

_____

_____

_____

7. Others believed that dragons were both masculine and feminine and added thirty-six scales. To include the feminine number six squared.

_____

_____

_____

_____

8. The most powerful dragons were the five-clawed variety. Which could be shown on decorations for the imperial house only.

_____

_____

_____

9. According to one early authority, dragons had the power to be visible or invisible at will. Cited by the Shuo Wen dictionary.

_____

_____

_____

10. They also had the power to change size. From a tiny being the size of a silkworm to an enormous presence. Filling the space between heaven and earth.

_____

_____

_____

_____

11. Transformations, too, were tricks dragons used. Making it difficult for people to study their behavior.

_____

_____

_____

12. To get a good look at a dragon, a person had to approach it at the right time. When it was asleep or thinking angry or lustful thoughts.

_____

_____

_____

_____

13. Sometimes dragons took human form. The most common choices were as old men or beautiful young women.

_____

_____

_____

14. One dragon, in female human form, is said to have joined the court of the emperor. To satisfy her desire to devour men.

_____

_____

_____

15. A Han dynasty emperor, who supposedly caught a dragon while fishing, had it served as a dinner dish. A delicacy of blue bones and purple flesh.

_____

_____

_____

_____

16. The bones and teeth of dragons ground into powder served as medicine. Which cured a variety of ailments, including fevers, gallstones, ulcers, paralysis, and boils.

_____

_____

_____

_____

17. These bones and teeth were probably the fossil remains of other ancient animals. Wherever they came from, they were extremely expensive.

_____

_____

_____

18. Doctors also recommended dragon brains, liver, skin, and fat. As powerful curative agents.

_____

_____

_____

19. Collecting dragon saliva, a substance which was valued as a perfume, often took years of patient waiting. To make sure the dragon had left his home and the saliva could be gathered safely.

_____

_____

_____

_____

20. Nowadays, the chief function of dragons is the symbolic decoration of manufactured items. Although some belief in dragons still persists.

_____

_____

_____

_____

NAME _____   DATE_____

EXERCISE 2: CORRECTING SENTENCE FRAGMENTS

Correct each of the following fragments either by attaching it to a main clause or by rewriting the fragment as a complete sentence. Mark correct items with a C.

EXAMPLE

In classical mythology dragons spring up everywhere. To threaten beautiful ladies and even whole communities.

In classical mythology dragons spring up everywhere to threaten beautiful ladies and even whole communities.

1. Hercules, possibly the greatest Greek hero, began his dragon killing early. Strangling two snakes just months after he was born.

   _____

   _____

   _____

   _____

2. As he grew to manhood, he performed many feats of strength and daring. And traveled throughout the Mediterranean area.

   _____

   _____

   _____

3. The priestess of Apollo told Hercules he could become immortal. As soon as he performed the labors assigned to him by Eurystheus.

   _____

   _____

   _____

   _____

4. One of the labors was to kill the Hydra. A water monster that lived in the swamps of Lerna.

_____

_____

_____

5. The Hydra supposedly had at least seven heads. Other versions of the story report as many as fifty thousand.

_____

_____

_____

6. Because its breath was poisonous and even the smell of its tracks could kill, it was impossible for Hercules to subdue it. Unless he held his breath for the entire fight.

_____

_____

_____

_____

7. Whenever Hercules struck off one of the Hydra's heads, two or three grew in its place. To complicate matters further.

_____

_____

_____

8. Hercules finally killed the Hydra with the help of a friend. Who set fire to a forest and burned each head stump, preventing any new growth.

_____

_____

_____

_____

9. Another notable dragon killer was Perseus. The son of the god Zeus and a beautiful but mortal woman, Danaë.

_____

_____

_____

10. Returning from his major triumph, the slaying of Medusa. Perseus heard that a certain King Cepheus had been forced to chain his beautiful daughter to a rock as an offering to a dragon who had been ravaging his land.

_____

_____

_____

_____

11. Perseus fell in love with the beautiful daughter, Andromeda. And promised the king to rescue her if he could marry her.

_____

_____

_____

12. Perseus apparently killed the dragon with ease. Because he had the help of a cap that made him invisible and a pair of winged sandals.

_____

_____

_____

_____

13. Arrangements were made for the wedding of Perseus and Andromeda over the objections of Phineus. Another suitor for Andromeda's hand.

_____

_____

_____

_____

14. Fortunately, Perseus had another valuable weapon with him. That he had saved from an earlier adventure.

_____

_____

_____

15. This weapon was the head of Medusa. It had the power to turn anyone who looked at it to stone, and Perseus always carried it with him. In a wallet draped over his shoulder.

_____

_____

_____

_____

16. As Phineus attacked Perseus. Perseus showed Medusa's head, and the wedding continued without further interruption.

_____

_____

_____

_____

17. Cadmus, unlike Hercules and Perseus, was not a son of Zeus. He was a formidable dragon killer nevertheless.

_____

_____

_____

18. While attempting to rescue his sister from the hands of Zeus. He came upon a ferocious dragon guarding the only available source of water.

_____

_____

_____

_____

19. After slaying the dragon, Cadmus sowed its teeth in the ground. On the advice of Athena. From the buried teeth sprang a whole army of soldiers.

_____

_____

_____

_____

20. Cadmus cleverly threw rocks among the soldiers, making each think he had been attacked by another. To prevent them from attacking him.

_____

_____

_____

_____

EXERCISE 3: CORRECTING COMMA SPLICES AND FUSED SENTENCES

Label each of the following items as correct (C), fused (FS), or containing a comma splice (CS). Correct the fused sentences and comma splices in any of the four ways mentioned in the text. Practice using all four ways instead of repeating the same correction each time.

EXAMPLE

Mozart started his study of music when he was only four years old, in a few years he had mastered the violin and the organ.

CS   Mozart started his study of music when he was only four years old. In a few years he had mastered the violin and the organ.

1. Mozart's work ranges from the simple to the most complicated, from the humorous to the tragic, and from the delicate to the heroic.

   Prepositional phrase

   CORRECT

   Sentence shows parallelism.
   ↳ cumulative effect

2. He completed an amazing number of works in a short life, he died at age thirty-five.

   CS.   He completed an amazing number of works in a short life, dying at age thirty-five.

3. Mozart was born in Salzburg, Austria, in 1756 his first performing tour was only six years later, in 1762.

   FS.   Mozart was born in Salzburg, Austria in 1756. His first performing tour was only six years later in 1762.

4. ~~His~~ *While Mozart's* father was a violinist, composer, and teacher, his sister was *also* an accomplished pianist.

   FS: _His father was a violinist, composer, and_
   teacher. His sister was an accomplished pianist.
   _____

5. The young Mozart traveled, on tour, to Italy, France, and England, the rulers of each country greeted him as a child genius.   *series*

   FS — The young Mozart traveled on to to Italy,
   France and England where the rulers of each
   country greated him as a child genius.

6. In Italy he was decorated by the pope, in England he wrote his first symphony.

   CS In Italy he was decorated by the pope. and
   In England he wrote his first symphony.
   _____

7. When Mozart first heard the string quartets of Haydn, he was so impressed with their beauty that he wrote six quartets of his own in a single month.

   Correct
   _____
   _____
   _____

8. Now a mature musician, Mozart served as concertmaster in a Salzburg orchestra on and off for ten years when he was in his mid twenties he won a commission to write an opera for a Munich carnival.

   f.S. Now a mature musican, Mozart served as concertmaster
   in a Salzburg orchestra on and off for ten years.
   When he was in his mid twenties, he won a commission
   to write an opera for a Munich carnival.

9. Opera was Mozart's favorite musical form, the piano was his favorite instrument.

cs *while* ~~Opera~~ was Mozart's favorite musical form, the piano was his favorite instrument.

10. *Don Giovanni* is considered by most critics to be his best opera his technique of using the orchestra to carry some of the emotion of the story was ahead of its time.

cs Don Giovanni is considered by most critics to be his best opera; his technique of using the orchestra to carry some of the emotion of the story was ahead of its time.

11. His three greatest symphonies were all written in the summer of 1788, when he was under great pressure to earn more money to support his family.

Correct

12. The following year he wrote three of his best string quartets, these were commissioned by the king of Prussia.

cs

13. Mozart never seemed to lack commissions, almost everything he composed was done on assignment for someone else.

cs   yet, because, since

14. One nobleman asked Mozart to compose a requiem mass in secret, he wanted to have the work performed as his own.

because

fs

_____

_____

_____

15. In spite of his great number of works and the acclaim they brought him, he was a poor man . when he died in 1791 he was buried in an unmarked grave.

and

fs

_____

_____

_____

squinting
modifier ← can go either
way.

EXERCISE 4: CORRECTING COMMA SPLICES AND FUSED SENTENCES

Correct the ten comma splices or fused sentences in the following paragraph, using the four methods of correction given in the text. The first one has been done as an example.

Diego Rivera, Mexico's famous revolutionary artist, created controversy throughout his life. His giant murals celebrating the cause of the working class were too radical for many people. A portrait of Lenin appeared in a mural he was painting at Rockefeller Center in New York City. In spite of a public outcry, he refused to remove it *however* he did offer to add a portrait of Abraham Lincoln. That wasn't enough, *consequently* His commission was canceled, *and* The unfinished mural was destroyed. He had lost this battle, however, he later challenged all the artistic *isms* of the early twentieth century. He disdained ordinary canvas-sized pictures. He believed that they inevitably end up in stuffy museums or the homes of the rich. Instead, he looked for huge walls on buildings where art could be used as a weapon in the class struggle. A typical Rivera mural is ablaze with color and full of people; it condemns exploitation of the masses or symbolizes the strength of purpose of awakened workers. Out of his sympathy for the poor, Rivera joined the Communist Party. He denounced the party in 1929 Then he was attacked by both leftists and rightists. He often carried a pistol for protection. When he died in 1957, controversy surrounded his funeral, too. The Communist Party covered his coffin with a red flag, Others opposed this gesture *and* fights erupted on the streets even as his body was lowered into the grave.

EXERCISE 5: CORRECTING ERRORS IN SUBJECT AND VERB AGREEMENT

In the following sentences, correct any errors in subject and verb agreement. If you find a correct sentence, mark it with a C.

EXAMPLE

Hank is one of the players who practice every day

1. Do not merely study English; study linguistics, which are connected to anthropology, psychology, and sociology as well as English.

2. From Alicia Munoz's pen comes images of mysterious journeys, questioning visitors, and relentless endurance tests.

3. *The Pickwick Papers*, first published as a serial, are a good example of Charles Dickens' genius as a caricaturist.

4. Kimmie is one of those people who dream of a future filled with fast cars and speed boats.

5. *Quizzes* are not as commonly misspelled as *existence*.

6. Every detective, desk sergeant, and traffic cop know the suspect has flaming red hair and a scarred cheek.

7. Porcupines exist around the world in numerous sizes and various shapes, but only one species exist in the United States.

8. There is a couple of wrong paths to the left.

9. Four pounds of beans are more than they can carry.

10. The battle of the sexes are composed of minute-to-minute encounters at home, on the streets, and in work places.

11. The preschool's giggling gang of three- and four-year olds love to chase the rabbits through the field.

12. At least once a week liver and onions are the main dish for an evening meal.

13. The gallery as well as the interior halls were redecorated before the tourist season.

14. A committee of students are meeting to discuss the library budget.

15. Neither the Department of State nor the visiting diplomats understand the reasons for the attack.

16. The creature prowling the moors makes loud music at night.

17. Both a school of piranhas and a great white shark is deadly to swimmers.

18. All but three of the projects has been completed on time.

19. Cycling in the park or hiking in the woods relax a person.

20. Everybody at the Smiths' were wearing a costume.

EXERCISE 6: SELECTING CORRECT PRONOUNS FOR PRONOUN AND ANTECEDENT AGREEMENT

Circle the correct pronoun for each sentence.

EXAMPLE

Neither the purse nor the pictures had (*its,* (*their*)) serial numbers intact.

1. Pearl's kitten, Bitsy, is the one (*that, who*) hid under the steps.

2. Either the ranger or the campers will report (*his, their*) findings to the Forest Service.

3. Everyone enjoyed (*his or her, their*) vacation at Oak Park.

4. Yoko, Rany, and Barbara received (*her, their*) class schedules in today's mail.

5. Yoko and Rany want to change (*hers, theirs*).

6. That group of musicians practiced (*its, their*) program every day.

7. Neither the salespeople nor the manager will receive (*his, their*) instructions on time.

8. The manager is the one (*that, who*) developed the sales strategy.

9. I believe Martha's dog, the one (*that, who*) won the best of show award, is a terrier.

10. Anyone (*who, that*) cares about grades will study every day.

11. Look for a blanket or comforter with a flower design on (*it, them*).

12. The committee proposed a solution at (*its, their*) last meeting.

13. Neither of the two routes is known for (*their, its*) lack of traffic.

14. The Academy of Fine Arts held (*its, their*) anniversary party last Friday.

15. The club adviser gave each of the girls (*her, their*) assignment.

16. Someone lost (*his or her, their*) glasses on the bus.

17. Every family in our neighborhood takes good care of (*its, their*) yard.

18. Both of the groups brought (*its, their*) own equipment.

19. A skier must select (*his or her, their*) equipment carefully.

20. Any bird (*who, that*) flies into our yard risks (*its, their*) life.

EXERCISE 7: SELECTING CORRECT PRONOUN CASE

For each of the following sentences, circle the correct case form.

EXAMPLE

Please pass the potatoes to (*I*, *me*)

1. (*She*, *Her*) and Irving went to the park together.

2. The post office offered (*she*, *her*) and (*me*, *I*) a summer job.

3. (*His*, *Him*) skating is a pleasure to watch.

4. The cooking was done by Pete and (*he*, *him*).

5. (*Whoever*, *Whomever*) lost the coat can claim it in the student union.

6. They have more trouble than (*we*, *us*).

7. The sudden change in weather left (*they*, *them*) stranded.

8. (*We*, *Us*) students can purchase theater tickets at a discount.

9. The best grade will be given to (*whoever*, *whomever*) designs the best poster.

10. (*Who*, *Whom*) is this picture for?

11. We discussed (*who*, *whom*) to take with (*we*, *us*).

12. Either Bob or (*I*, *me*) will represent the class at the conference.

13. (*Who Whom*) shall I say called?

14. You and (*I*, *me*) should go to the library to study.

15. I enjoyed (*you*, *your*) presenting the awards.

16. (*His*, *Him*) quick thinking won the debate.

17. (*Who*, *Whom*) promised to clean the room?

18. Why were (*they*, *them*) given so much attention?

19. The participants selected (*he*, *him*) and (*she*, *her*) to lead the parade.

20. I expected (*she*, *her*) to meet (*I*, *me*) at the station.

EXERCISE 8: SELECTING CORRECT VERB FORMS AND LEARNING PRINCIPAL PARTS OF VERBS

For each of the following sentences, circle the correct word from the pair in parentheses. On the three lines beneath each sentence, write the principal parts of the verb used in the sentence: infinitive, past, and past participle. Consult a dictionary if necessary.

EXAMPLE

Yesterday I (*lost* *losted*) my bus ticket.

lose _____ *lost* _____ *lost* _____

1. I (*did, done*) my homework early this week.

_____ _____ _____

2. The credit office finally (*found, founded*) my loan application.

_____ _____ _____

3. It's been a long time since I have (*heared, heard*) that song.

_____ _____ _____

4. Your bill has been (*payed, paid*).

_____ _____ _____

5. We should have (*bringed, brought*) some dessert.

_____ _____ _____

6. Last night Chris (*wore, worn*) her new outfit.

_____ _____ _____

7. Carrie slipped and (*fell, felled*) on the ice.

_____ _____ _____

8. The money has been safely (*hid, hidden*).

_____ _____ _____

9. I selected the pearls that had been (*gave, given*) to me by my grandmother.

_____   _____   _____

10. People were (*forbid, forbidden*) to enter the palace grounds.

_____   _____   _____

11. When the rain started, the children (*ran, ranned*) for cover.

_____   _____   _____

12. During the fight my shirt was (*tore, torn*) in three places.

_____   _____   _____

13. We have just (*began, begun*) to have fun!

_____   _____   _____

14. Brian fell off his skateboard and (*slid, slided*) all the way to the corner.

_____   _____   _____

15. By now the police should have (*catched, caught*) the burglar.

_____   _____   _____

16. When his hand slipped he (*cut, cutted*) the wrong piece.

_____   _____   _____

17. Yesterday I (*saw, seen*) an old friend from high school.

_____   _____   _____

18. For Christmas vacation they (*flew, flyed*) to Boston.

_____   _____   _____

19. The air was so cold it (*stinged, stung*) my face.

_____   _____   _____

20. I should have (*wrote, written*) earlier, but I lost your address.

_____   _____   _____

EXERCISE 9: CHANGING VERB TENSES

PART A   The following paragraph from *Manwatching: A Field Guide to Human Behavior*, by Desmond Morris, uses the present tense to discuss typical human reactions to crowds. Change the paragraph to make it refer to a period of time now past. The first sentence has been done as an example.

Of course, we all enjoy~~ed~~ the excitement of being in a crowd, and this reaction ~~cannot~~ *could not* be ignored. But there are crowds and crowds. It is pleasant enough to be in a "spectator crowd," but not so appealing to find yourself in the middle of a rush-hour crush. The difference between the two is that the spectator crowd is all facing in the same direction and concentrating on a distant point of interest. Attending a theatre, there are twinges of rising hostility toward the stranger who sits down immediately in front of you or the one who squeezes into the seat next to you. The shared armrest can become a polite, but distinct, territorial boundary-dispute region. However, as soon as the show begins, these invasions of Personal Space are forgotten and the attention is focused beyond the small space where the crowding is taking place. Now, each member of the audience feels himself spatially related, not to his cramped neighbors, but to the actor on the stage, and this distance is, if anything, too great. In the rush-hour crowd, by contrast, each member of the pushing throng is competing with his neighbors all the time. There is no escape to a spatial relation with a distant actor, only the pushing, shoving bodies all around.

PART B   The following paragraph, taken from a software review by Cheryl Goldberg in *PC*, is written in the present tense. Imagine that you are the developer of this as yet unwritten computer program. By changing the paragraph to the future tense, explain what your program will do when it is finished. The first two sentences have been done as examples.

The program ~~is~~ *will be* easy to use even without the tutorial. The main menu remain~~s~~ *will* at the top of

your screen at all times. You access seven pop-up submenus by hitting the Esc or slash (/) keys.

Once in a submenu, the program provides step-by-step instructions at the bottom of your screen,

prompting you through each menu operation. The Range menu allows you to create rectangles

and patterns, while Box commands are for drawing rectangles with thick, thin, dotted, or dou-

ble-line borders. The Ext commands permit enlarging, stretching, underlining, and boldfacing,

and Edit allows you to undo a command or create a backup file. File includes all file mainte-

nance operations. Print controls all printing operations including condensed type and multiple

copies. Quit requires you to confirm your intention to leave the program.

EXERCISE 10: SELECTING CORRECT TENSES IN SEQUENCE

Circle the verb form that is in sequence with the other verb or verbs in each of the following sentences.

EXAMPLE

He delighted in the games that his grandchildren (*play,* (*played*)).

1. The overworked assistants hope that the boss (*will be, would be*) absent tomorrow.

2. After the trial the attorneys relaxed in the cafeteria, confident that they (*won, had won*) the case.

3. As he whistled a happy song, he (*loads, loaded*) the heavy pack onto his shoulders.

4. I'm sorry. I know that I (*was, had been*) late yesterday.

5. The workers will strike because they (*believe, believed*) they are underpaid.

6. I will start on my political science project as soon as I (*will finish, have finished*) my composition.

7. The senator reads every letter from her constituents because she (*wants, wanted*) to keep in close contact with those who elected her.

8. The manager told us he (*has been, had been*) working there for twenty years.

9. I (*have been, had been*) walking until I bought my Kawasaki.

10. I think everyone will be tired after the dance (*is, was*) over.

EXERCISE 11: USING ACTIVE AND PASSIVE VOICE

PART A   All of the following sentences are written in passive voice. Explain why the passive voice is appropriate in each case.

EXAMPLE

Amos was surprised by the warmth of the reception.

Emphasizes the receiver of the action.

1. The warehouse was destroyed by the fire.

   _____

2. Fortunately, or suspiciously, the paintings had been removed the day before.

   _____

3. One woman was seriously burned by falling cinders.

   _____

4. She was rushed to the emergency room by the paramedics.

   _____

5. "The fire was set deliberately," the fire chief reported.

   _____

PART B   Change each passive construction in the following sentences to an active construction. If there are no passive constructions in a sentence, mark it A.

EXAMPLE

Copies of the proposed rules were provided by the safety committee.

The safety committee provided copies of the proposed rules.

6. The repairs on my automobile were done by inexperienced mechanics.

   _____

   _____

7. A detailed rendering was submitted by the architect.

_____

_____

8. This essay was written by me.

_____

_____

9. The TV program *Cheers* received many awards.

_____

_____

10. Many stargazers were disappointed by Halley's comet.

_____

_____

11. The new guidelines were approved by the executive committee.

_____

_____

12. A small chip of wood was removed from his eye by the doctor.

_____

_____

13. Good writers use passive voice sparingly.

_____

_____

14. I do not like to get up too early in the morning.

_____

_____

15. Do you know if the dinner is going to be served by the Ski Club?

_____

_____

16. When the cleanup crew arrived, the picnic grounds were covered with litter.

_____

_____

17. Raise the bowl carefully to avoid spilling the liquid.

_____

_____

18. The first-place trophy was won by Kim's home movie.

_____

_____

19. The game was won with a last-minute desperation shot by Gary Richards.

_____

_____

20. Let the chips fall where they may.

_____

_____

EXERCISE 12: USING ADJECTIVES AND ADVERBS

For each of the following sentences, select the correct modifier from the pair in parentheses and write it on the first blank below the sentence. In the second blank, identify the modifier as either an adjective or an adverb. In the third blank, write the word or words it modifies.

EXAMPLE

Time capsules are an (*interesting, interestingly*) attempt to communicate with future generations.

interesting _____ *adjective* _____ *attempt* _____

1. Creating and burying time capsules has been a (*popular, popularly*) community activity in the United States for over a hundred years.

   _____   _____   _____

2. (*Unfortunate, Unfortunately*), most time capsules buried during those hundred years can no longer be located.

   _____   _____   _____

3. One expert (*cautious, cautiously*) estimates that over 5,000 have been buried and 60 percent will never be found.

   _____   _____   _____

4. Although those who bury such capsules mean (*good, well*), too often they make no provision for any (*permanent, permanently*) above-ground record of the capsule's location.

   _____   _____   _____

   _____   _____   _____

5. As a result, some capsules are dug up (*unintentional, unintentionally*) before their time and others cannot be located even when the time is up.

   _____   _____   _____

6. Los Angeles nearly lost a capsule buried in 1976; a newspaper reporter had (*considerable, considerably*) difficulty locating it only nine years later.

   _____   _____   _____

7. Even the person who had done public relations (*specific, specifically*) for the capsule had forgotten where it was.

   _____ _____ _____

8. The reporter finally found the capsule by reading newspaper clippings from the (*early, earlier*) time.

   _____ _____ _____

9. The (*funnier, funniest*) case of all was the capsule that had to be dug up only three years after it was buried.

   _____ _____ _____

10. A group of citizens insisted (*loud, loudly*) that a book of ethnic jokes be removed at once.

    _____ _____ _____

11. The (*larger, largest*) time capsule is really an abandoned gold mine in Lancaster, California, scheduled to be opened in 2866.

    _____ _____ _____

12. In his front yard in Nebraska, one man buried a suit of clothes, some bikini panties, a motorcycle, and a Chevrolet Vega, making his capsule perhaps the (*most expensive, expensivest*) in the United States.

    _____ _____ _____

13. Corona, California, has the (*baddest, worst*) record for losing capsules; seventeen capsules have been misplaced there.

    _____ _____ _____

14. Time capsules now are being made with (*better, best*) material than before.

    _____ _____ _____

15. (*Special, Specially*) designed capsules within capsules should even survive earthquakes (*safe, safely*).

    _____ _____ _____

    _____ _____ _____

16. In the future those responsible for burying capsules will (*sure, surely*) keep better records.

_____   _____   _____

17. Some have (*recent, recently*) suggested that a (*concentrated, concentratedly*) effort be made to build a national capsule registry.

_____   _____   _____

_____   _____   _____

18. Have you ever thought (*serious, seriously*) about what you would put in a time capsule?

_____   _____   _____

19. Some people, for example, would feel (*uneasy, uneasily*) about having future generations look at their personal diaries.

_____   _____   _____

20. Others would feel (*perfect, perfectly*) happy about it.

_____   _____   _____

EXERCISE 1: USING COORDINATION AND SUBORDINATION

Rewrite each of the following pairs of sentences, using coordination and subordination. Make each sentence clear and logical.

EXAMPLE

I opened the front door. My dog ran to greet me.

When I opened the front door, my dog ran to greet me. _____

1. Shirley rides a bicycle. She comes home from school fifteen minutes before James.

   _____

   _____

2. Read the newspaper. You will learn about politics.

   _____

   _____

3. Max wanted to learn French. Max went to Paris.

   _____

   _____

4. One of my aunts lives in San Francisco. She teaches psychology.

   _____

   _____

5. A strong odor came from beneath his house. The police chief was suspicious.

   _____

   _____

6. She moved to another part of the city. She would be closer to her work.

_____

_____

7. Bobby Joe was cooking dinner. The phone rang.

_____

_____

8. Yung was tired. He had been looking all over town for his dog.

_____

_____

9. I turn on the television. I see a commercial first.

_____

_____

10. You are going to the grocery store. Buy me some gum.

_____

_____

EXERCISE 2: CORRECTING EXCESSIVE COORDINATION AND SUBORDINATION

Each of the following sentences contains excessive coordination or subordination. Rewrite the sentences, making them both clear and logical. Omit irrelevant detail. You may need to write more than one sentence for some of the originals.

EXAMPLE

Dr. Randolf, who was born and who went to dental school in Omaha, Nebraska, one of the fine midwestern cities, that is famous for its steak restaurants, said that he would like to move back there someday because he is homesick and he misses the city.

Dr. Randolf, a dentist, said he would like to move back to Omaha, Nebraska, someday because he was homesick.

1. Our dog ran away, and the cat that lived next door disappeared, and some of the neighbors believe that there is a connection.

   _____

   _____

   _____

2. No one has seen the dog and cat for three days, yet Mr. Withers and Ms. Conrad, who seem to be seeing a lot of each other these days, since Mr. Withers moved into the house that Orville Whittaker built, insist that the dog and cat will both return.

   _____

   _____

   _____

   _____

   _____

3. Mr. Withers works in the local furrier's, which is not so busy as it was last year, and Ms. Conrad works in the local pet food factory, where she is an accountant, and both of them drive to work in the same car because they want to save money.

_____

_____

_____

_____

4. After Ms. Conrad arrives at the pet food factory, which stands near the corner of Murfton Avenue and Siegfried Street, she begins her day by turning on the photocopy machine that stands just outside her office, and then she turns on her computer.

_____

_____

_____

_____

5. Mr. Withers, who drops off Ms. Conrad at the pet food factory, begins his day at the furrier's by brushing six or seven fur coats so that they will be fluffy.

_____

_____

_____

6. The furs that are for sale at the furrier's where Mr. Withers works are expensive, and they are made from an acrylic and polyester combination, which makes them look real.

_____

_____

_____

7. Many of our nearby neighbors, who have been living near us for many years, have organized a nightly search party for our missing dog and cat, who both disappeared at about the same time, and they walk all over the area.

_____

_____

_____

_____

8. The cat, whose name is Butch, and the dog, whose name is Mimi, have never been good friends, which is why no one believes that they suddenly decided to leave whenever they thought they had a chance, like pets leave in television cartoons on Saturday mornings.

_____

_____

_____

_____

9. Pets, when you first bring them home, are enjoyable, especially if they are frisky, like a puppy or a kitten, but when you realize how much time it takes to care for a pet properly, sometimes you lose interest in their welfare.

_____

_____

_____

_____

10. Calvin's old dog lies around the house all day, and his pet snake silently slides through the house nightly, yet his pet hamster exercises happily in his cage, unaware of the dangers just beyond his wire enclosure.

_____

_____

_____

_____

EXERCLSE 3: PLACING MODIFIERS

Recast the following sentences so that they illustrate clear writing. Some sentences have more than one error.

EXAMPLE

Mr. Winter, after looking all over the campus for the student who had told him that she wanted to enroll in his class, sighed.

After looking all over the campus for the student who had told him she wanted to enroll in his class, Mr. Winter sighed.

1. Denton Cooley, once an assistant in many heart operations and now a world-famous heart surgeon in his own right, estimates that he has at least performed 65,000 heart operations.

_____

_____

_____

_____

2. He has one of the lowest mortality rates anywhere of any heart surgeon.

_____

_____

3. He has nearly performed ninety-one heart transplants.

_____

_____

4. Dr. Cooley also developed and implanted first the temporary heart.

_____

_____

5. His career includes, among a number of adventures and awards so richly deserved, doing the world's first heart operation.

_____

_____

_____

6. He in the mid-1950s invented one of the early heart-lung machines.

_____

_____

7. In excess of $20 million, he has amassed a personal fortune.

_____

_____

_____

8. In early December 1967, Dr. Christiaan Barnard, Cooley heard on the radio, had done the first human heart transplant.

_____

_____

_____

9. Cooley was, like most surgeons, dumfounded.

_____

_____

10. Cooley, by the courage of Dr. Barnard, was stimulated.

_____

_____

EXERCISE 4: CORRECTING FAULTY PRONOUN REFERENCE

Correct the faulty pronoun references in the following sentences. You may have to change words or recast entire sentences.

EXAMPLE

Alicia owned a dog and a rabbit but it died.

Alicia owned a dog and a rabbit, but the dog died.

They audited Eddie's income tax return.

The Internal Revenue Service audited Eddie's income tax return.

1. It is necessary that we build a new foundation for our statue of General Martinet. It is crumbling.

   _____

   _____

   _____

2. The statue has stood in the park for more than fifty years, and it is crowded every Fourth of July.

   _____

   _____

   _____

3. They should have arrested the people who poked holes in the statue's weak foundation.

   _____

   _____

   _____

4. The statue looks as if he will collapse any minute.

   _____

   _____

5. If the statue falls when people are around and pieces of it fly through the air, some of them may be hurt.

_____

_____

_____

6. The city council told the citizens that they can help to rebuild it.

_____

_____

7. Time is passing, and no one is doing anything about it.

_____

_____

8. If the foundation is not replaced before the next Fourth of July, it may not be a happy celebration because it may collapse.

_____

_____

_____

9. If General Martinet's statue collapses, they will have no reason to visit the park.

_____

_____

_____

10. It could happen because nobody seems too interested.

_____

_____

EXERCISE 5: CORRECTING FAULTY SHIFTS

Recast each of the following sentences so that it no longer has any inconsistencies.

EXAMPLE

In one of the technical reports said that plastic could never be used to make engine parts.

One of the technical reports said that plastic could never be used to make engine parts.

1. In 60 percent of a new engine is made of plastic.

_____

_____

2. By using plastic makes the engine lightweight.

_____

_____

3. The engine can sit in a child's wagon, and the wagon can be easily pulled by them.

_____

_____

4. When a child does pull the wagon loaded with the powerful engine, they feel proud.

_____

_____

5. The new engine is called the Polimotor, and they were designed by Matthew Holtzberg.

_____

_____

6. When Holtzberg spoke to a recent engineers' meeting, he spoke calmly, saying most of the engine's moving parts are made of Torlon, and he also said that Torlon is a heat-resistant plastic resin.

_____

_____

_____

_____

7. In the engine block itself is made of a graphite-fabric and epoxy composite.

_____

_____

8. In the future is when drivers will have fewer mechanical problems because of their Polimotors.

_____

_____

9. According to Holtzberg, the first question everyone asks when they see a plastic engine is why the thing doesn't melt?

_____

_____

_____

10. Holtzberg tells people that metal was put by engineers where the greatest heat is generated.

_____

_____

EXERCISE 6: MAKING SENTENCES LOGICALLY COMPLETE

Recast the following sentences to complete all comparisons logically and to correct all faulty ellipses fully.

EXAMPLE

After I graduate, I would like to visit someday.

After I graduate from Central State College, I would like to visit the school someday.

1. Our car is so old.

   _____

   _____

2. When our car was new, it averaged thirty miles per gallon; now, twenty.

   _____

   _____

3. We would trade in our car, except for the expense.

   _____

   _____

4. No new-car dealer wants our old clunker; our total down payment is cash instead.

   _____

   _____

5. We went to the Ford dealer; then to Chevrolet.

   _____

   _____

6. They both said our car is too old.

_____

_____

7. Our town has more old cars than any town in the country.

_____

_____

8. Compared with some of them, ours is not so bad.

_____

_____

9. Our car just looks old and ugly compared with new cars.

_____

_____

10. Someday, our car won't get us there.

_____

_____

EXERCISE 7: CORRECTING FAULTY PARALLELISM

Correct faulty parallelism in the following sentences.

EXAMPLE

Walking rapidly for five minutes burns fewer calories than a five-minute jog.

Walking rapidly for five minutes burns fewer calories

than jogging for five minutes.

1. Athletes develop exceptional muscle tone, unusual lung capacity, and ~~they have~~ healthy mental attitudes.

   _____

   _____

   _____

2. Coaches aid athletes by helping them both physically and with their emotions.

   Coaches aid athletes by helping them both

   physically & emotionally.

   _____

3. Aerobics helps the lungs, the heart, and ~~is good for~~ the muscles~~, too~~.

   _____

   _____

4. Many athletes train with aerobics and ~~using~~ weights.

   _____

   _____

5. Aerobic training builds endurance, and weight training is good for building muscles.

Aerobic training builds endurance, while weight

training bu

6. Second-rate athletes are often found on the sidelines, or bench-warming.

7. Some athletes refusing to exercise are the same athletes who want playing time.

wanting

8. Coaches occasionally do not know whether to permit an athlete to play or if they should require that an athlete practice more.

to

9. All coaches like to see their athletes play hard, win often, and to enjoy a successful season.

10. After a particularly rough game, many athletes enjoy going to a party, to relaxing among friends, or to stay home to watch a late-night movie on television .

Staying

EXERCISE 8: IDENTIFYING SENTENCE STRUCTURES AND FORMS

Each of the following sentences is followed by two words, one of which more accurately describes the sentence, either in terms of its *structure* or in terms of its *form*. Underline the word that more accurately describes each sentence.

EXAMPLE

After she arrived at work, Joanne realized she had locked her dog in the bathroom.

[loose   complex]

1. The Department of Energy (DOE) is developing an interesting way to process radioactive and toxic waste that has already been buried.   [periodic   complex]

2. The DOE melts it and turns it and the surrounding soil into a glass-like block.

   [loose   compound]

3. The DOE workers drive four carbon electrodes into the ground.   [loose   compound]

4. The workers connect each electrode to a power source.   [periodic   simple]

5. They then release a strong electric current, which passes through the soil between the electrodes.   [loose   compound]

6. The temperature of the soil reaches 1,300 to 1,500 degrees Fahrenheit almost immediately, melting the waste, rock, and earth.   [loose   complex]

7. Slowly and evenly through the "soup," the waste is distributed.   [complex   periodic]

8. A cover traps escaping gases, and the cover draws those gases into purifying equipment.

   [periodic   compound]

9. When the soup cools into a solid block, it looks like a black rock.   [compound   periodic]

10. Scientists have said that the block is more durable than granite.   [simple   periodic]

11. The mass shrinks as it melts. [loose   compound]

12. After it cools, the mass can be covered with topsoil. [loose   complex]

13. Experiments suggest that large equipment could produce cubes that are 20 feet per side and that weigh 400 tons. [compound   loose]

14. One researcher said that this process encapsulates radioactivity. [complex   periodic]

15. The new process may be more economical than burying waste, but the process requires more testing. [periodic   compound]

16. Often, scientists discover how to rid our environment of waste, but occasionally scientists are stumped for answers. [compound   periodic]

17. Polluted areas must be discovered before they can be cleaned up. [loose   compound]

18. After the polluted areas are discovered, the proper authorities are notified.

    [compound   periodic]

19. First, authorities are alerted, and then scientists are notified. [complex   balanced]

20. The public and the politicians should work together to see that our environment remains relatively safe. [compound   loose]

EXERCISE 1: USING COMMAS WITH COORDINATING CONJUNCTIONS LINKING MAIN CLAUSES

Insert a comma at each place in the following sentences where one is required. If a sentence is correct, mark it with a C in the left-hand margin.

EXAMPLE

Most of us ignore the development of words͵yet their development is often revealing.

1. Some words are unacceptable and should never be uttered yet the history of these words shows that they have legitimate beginnings.

2. *Ain't* is such a word and some linguists claim it is a very good and useful word.

3. The use of *ain't* began in England in 1706 and the word was soon used in America.

4. *Ain't* developed as a contraction of *am not* so it was first spelled *an't*.

5. In 1778-79 *an't* had become *ain't* on both sides of the Atlantic but some New Englanders still pronounced it with a broad *a* like *an't*.

6. By the 1830s *ain't* was still used but many people had begun to misuse it.

7. *Ain't* was an obvious contraction of *am not* yet people began to use it as a contraction for *is not* and *are not* also.

8. Educated people began to criticize its common use for they believed it was unacceptable in all its forms.

9. Teachers say we are not supposed to use *ain't* anymore yet people still use it.

10. The educated use it with a self-conscious smirk and the uneducated use it naturally.

EXERCISE 2: USING COMMAS WITH INTRODUCTORY PHRASES AND CLAUSES

Insert commas where needed after introductory phrases and clauses in the following sentences. If a sentence is correct, mark it with a C in the left-hand margin.

EXAMPLE

When it comes to derring-do performances on film, most movie-goers think of stunt men.

1. In the past dangerous movie stunts were performed only by men.

2. Dressed as women men even performed stunts for leading ladies.

3. Although men still perform most stunts there is a growing number of stunt women.

4. In spite of early Hollywood resistance stunt women do everything from rolling cars at 70 MPH to leaping from helicopters.

5. At 5-foot-3 with a slim 105-pound frame Simone Boisserer is one of Hollywood's leading stunt women.

6. Like a ballerina she moves with grace and precision.

7. Training as a ski instructor and rodeo performer gave Boisserer the agility and courage the job requires.

8. Pressing the gas pedal to the floor she once drove a car off a ferryboat and plowed into another car.

9. Before the dust cleared she stepped from the wreckage with her front teeth missing and began to prepare for her next performance.

10. When asked what being a stunt woman is like she said it is something like being a kamikaze pilot.

EXERCISE 3: WRITING SENTENCES WITH INTRODUCTORY PHRASES
AND CLAUSES

Select an article from a leading newspaper or magazine. Read the article; then write ten sentences, each beginning with an introductory clause or phrase, as indicated in each of the following items.

EXAMPLE

Introductory clause beginning with *although*.

Although the situation is tense, no one has fired a shot.

1. Introductory clause beginning with *when*.

   _____

   _____

2. Introductory prepositional phrase beginning with *in*.

   _____

   _____

3. Introductory verbal phrase beginning with *driving*.

   _____

   _____

4. Introductory clause beginning with *after* or *before*.

   _____

   _____

5. Introductory prepositional phrase beginning with *during*.

   _____

   _____

For the following five items, select your own beginning word.

6. Introductory verbal phrase.

_____

_____

7. Introductory clause.

_____

_____

8. Introductory prepositional phrase.

_____

_____

9. Introductory verbal clause.

_____

_____

10. Introductory prepositional phrase.

_____

_____

EXERCISE 4: USING COMMAS TO SET OFF NONRESTRICTIVE ELEMENTS

In the following sentences, insert commas to set off nonrestrictive clauses, phrases, and appositives. If a sentence is correct as written, underline the restrictive or nonrestrictive element and mark the sentence with a C.

EXAMPLE

Everyone who has a taste for curious events and methodical investigation must read mystery

fiction which has a 250-year history.

1. The Beat poets like wandering troubadours would read their poetry to any audience that

   would listen.

2. True vegetarians will not eat food that has a central nervous system.

3. The Pulitzer Prize is one award journalists throughout the United States covet.

4. Actors James Cagney and George Raft both of whom began their careers as dancers became

   famous because of movie roles as gangsters in the 1930s.

5. Anxious law students often study sixty to seventy hours a week which could jeopardize their

   health.

6. Anyone who has the time and patience can learn to play a musical instrument.

7. Thomas Pynchon's novel *The Crying of Lot 49* embodies a conspiratorial vision of America.

8. Fabian whose full name is Fabian Anthony Forte was a 1950s teen idol.

9. Our army traveling under the cover of darkness arrived at the bridge undetected.

10. In 1986 hundreds of peace advocates who came from every segment of American society

    marched from Los Angeles to Washington, D. C. to promote world disarmament a goal mil-

    lions of ordinary citizens are still working to achieve.

EXERCISE 5: COMBINING SENTENCES

Combine the following sentences according to the directions given in brackets. After you have combined the sentences, be sure to punctuate them correctly.

EXAMPLE

Of all the crusades, the Children's Crusade shocks us the most. It produced nearly fifty thousand casualties. [Use an adjective clause]

Of all the crusades, the Children's Crusade, which produced nearly fifty thousand casualties, shocks us the most.

1. The crowd gathered at the palace gates. It listened to the voice coming over the loudspeaker. [Use a participial phrase.]

_____

_____

2. The senior class purchased a new scoreboard for the school. Its members were the rowdiest in the school's history. [Use an adjective clause.]

_____

_____

3. The go-away bird gets its nickname from a call that sounds human. This bird is actually a gray loerie. [Use an appositive.]

_____

_____

4. The old man sat in the back row. He collapsed when the race started. [Use a participial phrase.]

_____

_____

5. Holographic images appear to be three-dimensional. They are created by laser beams. [Use an adjective clause.]

_____

_____

6. Western Samoa has 160,000 inhabitants. My mother was born there. [Use an adjective clause.]

_____

_____

7. Roman invasions brought Britain into contact with the Continent. The invading legions struck in the first century B.C. [Use a participial phrase.]

_____

_____

8. Winston Churchill and Franklin Roosevelt agreed to force Adolf Hitler to surrender unconditionally. Their meeting took place in Morocco. [Use a prepositional phrase.]

_____

_____

9. The central character, John Blackthorne, survives a grueling incarceration. He is shipwrecked in feudal Japan. [Use an adverb clause.]

_____

_____

10. Stephen Crane wrote The Red Badge of Courage. It is a novel about a soldier in the American Civil War. Crane had never been a soldier himself. [Use an adjective clause and an appositive.]

_____

_____

_____

EXERCISE 6: USING COMMAS TO SET OFF PARENTHETICAL EXPRESSIONS AND MILD INTERJECTIONS

Insert commas as necessary to set off parenthetical expressions and mild interjections in the following sentences. If a sentence is correct, mark it with a C in the left-hand margin.

EXAMPLE

The macabre, no doubt, fascinates you; I, therefore, will tell you about vampires.

1. Vampire legends have developed in countries around the world; moreover the tales have the same fundamental characteristics everywhere.

2. All vampires for example leave their graves at night; furthermore they must return to the graves by dawn.

3. Of course as you well know vampires live on human blood, and according to tradition a vampire can be killed by driving a stake through its heart.

4. Yes garlic always drives a hungry vampire away, but a cross to most people's surprise doesn't always work.

5. Some experts claim that vampires are suicides; however a larger number claim anyone under a vampire curse will become a victim.

6. Still others say that the seventh son of a seventh son is always a vampire; all experts agree however that anyone who survives a vampire bite becomes a vampire.

7. However vampires are created, they have been in our lore for over five hundred years.

8. In fact novelist Bram Stoker's Count Dracula was named after a historic figure, Prince Vlad Tepes; the prince unfortunately was as bloodthirsty as Stoker's imaginary count.

9. Hollywood has been creating vampire stories since the days of silent films, but some vampire-film buffs claim the image of the heartless vampire was softened by a humorous vampire movie named *Love at First Bite*.

10. Do you believe vampires actually exist? Probably not but we must have imaginary creatures that go thump in the night; otherwise life would lose some of its innocent terror.

EXERCISE 7: USING COMMAS IN A SERIES AND BETWEEN
COORDINATE ADJECTIVES

Insert commas as necessary within a series or between coordinate adjectives in the following sentences. Include the last comma in a series. If a sentence is correct, mark it with a C in the left-hand margin.

EXAMPLE

Spanish conquistador Hernando Cortés invaded the Aztec Empire in 1519 enslaved the native

population and began the Spanish plunder of the New World.

1. Most people were farmers or worked for small local businesses, often bartering food clothing and services.

2. A third of the country was poorly housed poorly dressed poorly fed.

3. Driven from their native land by the potato famine, a million hungry uneducated immigrants came to America during the 1840s.

4. The immigrants arrived in New York, soon moved north to Boston and south to Philadelphia and then trekked west toward California.

5. Following the Revolutionary war, far-sighted courageous leaders like Benjamin Franklin, George Washington, Robert Fulton, and Albert Gallatin planned to build canals to connect towns lakes and rivers across the new nation.

6. The first plane flight in America took place in 1903—the Wright brothers' 120-foot 12-second historic ride.

7. During the California gold rush, easterners quit their jobs abandoned their families and ignored their common sense for the chance to go west and strike it rich.

8. The catfish bald eagle rattlesnake and hummingbird were given their vivid names because of an outstanding characteristic: whiskers like a cat a head of white feathers a rattle like a child's toy and wings that hum in flight.

9. At the peak of the Great Depression, bank closings bankruptcies factory shutdowns and farm and home mortgage foreclosures were at an all-time high.

10. With mustard and relish and onions, the American hot dog has been the favorite of Fourth of July picnics for one hundred years.

EXERCISE 8: USING COMMAS TO SET OFF CERTAIN EXPRESSIONS, INTERROGATIVE ELEMENTS, AND EXPLANATORY WORDS USED WITH DIRECT QUOTATIONS

Insert commas as necessary in the following sentences to set off absolute phrases, contrasting expressions, interrogative elements, and explanatory words used with direct quotations. If a sentence is correct, mark it with a C in the left-hand margin.

EXAMPLE

Overeating as opposed to excessive smoking and drinking might be the secret of a short life.

1. "Americans" reports one health expert "have always associated an affluent lifestyle with a diet heavy in fat and sugar."

2. "Mix fat and sugar with large quantities of salt and the diet will kill you" one nutritionist claims.

3. Commercial meat, an American diet staple, is highly suspect not just because of the fat and cholesterol.

4. Whenever you bite into a hamburger or leg of lamb, along with the seasoning you are probably getting generous helpings of everything from growth hormones not for your growth but for the animal's to printer's ink from paper recycled into feed for fiber.

5. Not an appetizing thought is it?

6. One rancher actually asked "Why should city folk worry about chemicals in their meat?" He continued "They use chemical sanitizers, insecticides, and tranquilizers don't they?"

7. "You bet, but consumers *choose* to use them!" one outraged nutritionist responded.

8. "Chemicals are becoming so widely used in cattle raising that consumers might soon need a prescription to buy a hamburger" one critic joked.

9. Chemicals not just the high cost of meat are one reason health-conscious people are turning to fish.

10. The sushi bar in contrast to the steak house is the latest success story in American dining.

EXERCISE 9: COMMA REVIEW 1

Correct the following sentences by inserting commas where they are needed. Include all optional commas. If any sentence is correct, mark it with a C in the left-hand margin.

EXAMPLE

Just because you bought an item that turns out to be a lemon, do not feel that you have to put up with it.

1. As a result of the consumer movement of the 1970s most firms now have a consumer department to help with problems.

2. Sometimes though the red tape involved in resolving a complaint can seem endless; however there are certain ways to complain that get results.

3. First follow up every meeting or phone call with a typewritten letter.

4. The letter should look businesslike not like hastily scrawled lecture notes if it is to impress its recipient and the tone should not sound angry.

5. Second if your efforts at the local level or point of purchase are unsuccessful most consumer service experts suggest you write to the regional director if the company involved is large enough to have one.

6. In addition send one copy of your letter to the firm's president and other copies to the local Better Business Bureau and the state or local consumer protection office.

7. Be sure to include your name and address and home and work telephone numbers in your letter.

8. You should also include the model and serial number of the item a description and history of the problem and copies of all pertinent documents such as sales slips and warranty details.

9. End your letter by requesting a response within a reasonable period usually two weeks which will give a supervisor plenty of time to investigate your complaint.

10. If you do not get a response within two weeks send a follow-up registered letter requesting details on what is being done about your complaint and include a copy of your original letter.

11. Telephone companies have been the target of complaining customers since the breakup of AT&T in 1984.

12. Back in the old days all you had to do was call Ma Bell (from an outside phone of course) when the phone went on the fritz.

13. Now when you buy your own phone you are responsible for its maintenance and since consumers are learning that some of the new inexpensive telephones cannot handle much abuse many find it is cheaper to buy a new phone than to get one repaired.

14. One telephone repairman claims "Most common phone problems contrary to popular thinking can be avoided" but he offers no official advice.

15. "Just use plain common sense" he adds "and a little simple maintenance."

16. You should not for instance drop your telephone for the striker might catch under the bell assembly or the dial tone buttons might stick.

17. After dropping your phone, you might begin to get wrong numbers a discouraging experience if the error happens frequently.

18. Because of damage from the fall the finger stop on the rotary dial might be stuck against the dial preventing smooth dialing and causing wrong numbers.

19. Remember that you can take off the outside case and use a screwdriver to loosen the striker or wrench free a stuck button or pry up the finger stop; after all it is your telephone right?

20. This is just simple maintenance the kind anyone can perform.

EXERCISE 10: COMMA REVIEW 2

Correct the following sentences by inserting commas where they are needed and deleting them where they are not needed. Include all optional commas. If any sentence is correct, mark it with a C in the left-hand margin.

EXAMPLE

Myths, folk tales, and fables have always been used, by humankind to convey life's lessons.

1. "The Boy Who Drew Cats" a Japanese tale offers a lesson on the power of art.

2. A clever young boy was left by his father who was a farmer at the village temple to become a priest because he was weak and small and people said he would never grow big enough to be a farmer himself.

3. A wise old priest agreed to take the boy as an acolyte, and to educate him for the priesthood.

4. The boy learned quickly what the old priest taught him and was obedient in most things but he had one fault.

5. He liked to draw cats during his study hours and he even drew cats where cats ought not to have been drawn at all.

6. He drew them on the margins of the priest's books and on all the screens of the temple and on all the walls and pillars.

7. Although the priest told him this was not right the boy did not stop drawing cats; moreover he drew all the more loving his art more than his studies.

8. Acolytes are supposed to study not draw so the wise yet stern priest said "You must leave the temple!", which really made the priest sad inside. Then he leaned toward the boy. "Avoid large places" he warned holding up a finger "keep to small places."

9. The boy did not know what the priest meant by saying "Avoid large places; keep to small places."

10. He thought and thought while he was tying up his little bundle of clothes to go away, but he could not understand the priest's words, and he was afraid to speak to the priest any more except to say good-by.

11. Disappointed and sorrowful he left the temple wondering what he should do.

12. If he went straight home he felt his father would punish him for having been disobedient to the priest so he decided to go to another temple in a distant village.

13. But unfortunately he did not know that the temple was closed, and that the priests had been frightened away by a bloodthirsty goblin so fierce that many brave warriors had been unable to defeat it.

14. He approached the temple but heard no sound coming from inside. He entered but found no priest.

15. Then he noticed that everything in the temple was covered by a thick, gray dust.

16. "They must need an acolyte" the boy said to himself "to keep the temple clean."

17. What most pleased him however were big white screens which would be good to paint cats on.

18. Even though he was tired he looked at once for a writing box found one with ink and began to paint cats.

19. After painting many cats upon the screens he began to feel tired his eyes growing heavy with sleep.

20. He decided to lie down beside one of the screens but he remembered the priest's words "Avoid large places; keep to small places."

21. The temple was very large and he was all alone. Without understanding why he began to feel afraid.

22. Glancing about the temple he looked for a small place for him to squeeze into.

23. He found one a small cabinet near the cats he had painted on the screen crawled in and fell fast asleep.

24. Very late in the night he was awakened by a terribly violent noise, a noise of fighting and screaming.

25. The noise was so dreadful that he was afraid even to look through a chink in the little cabinet; instead he lay very still holding his breath.

26. Even when a long silence came, the boy was afraid his life was in danger.

27. Finally he crawled cautiously from his hiding place and looked around.

28. First he saw that the temple floor was covered with blood. Next he saw lying dead in the middle of it an enormous rat a goblin that was bigger than a cow.

29. "But who or what killed it?" he wondered. Suddenly the boy saw that the mouths and claws of the cats he had drawn were red and wet with blood .

30. Years later the boy became a very famous artist and some of the cats he drew are still shown to travelers in Japan.

EXERCISE 11: USING SEMICOLONS

Delete the unnecessary and incorrect commas and semicolons and insert the correct punctuation in the following sentences. If any sentence is correct, mark it with a C in the left-hand margin.

EXAMPLE

Report after report documents the dangers of caffeine⁄consequently, more Americans seem to

be cutting down on coffee consumption.

1. Many Americans are dropping coffee completely from their diets, many others are switching to decaffeinated coffee.

2. Herbal teas or health-food substitutes are reasonable alternatives to coffee drinking, they are drunk hot and offer a reason to pause during the day.

3. "I have measured out my life with coffee spoons," the poet T. S. Eliot once wrote, now, however, he might have to write, "I have measured out my life with teaspoons."

4. Coffee has been nicknamed "mud"; because the grounds look like mud once hot water has been poured through them.

5. Some people drink as much as fifteen to twenty cups of coffee a day; which makes sleeping difficult because of the caffeine.

6. Some people drink coffee to stay alert, then they cannot sleep, finally, they drink coffee the next morning because they are tired from the lack of sleep.

7. Many heavy coffee drinkers who finally quit drinking coffee experience the symptoms of withdrawal; such as headaches, depression, and listlessness.

8. Is there life after coffee consumption has ended? Coffee drinking is such a ritualized part of our experience that giving up coffee would disrupt our schedules, in fact, giving up coffee might change the very fabric of our existence.

9. Imagine having herbal tea with eggs and bacon, sipping caffeineless cola with the morning paper, taking juice breaks, without coffee all these experiences would be equally dissatisfying.

10. Improved health is not worth the emotional price tag; coffee is the one drink for all occasions.

EXERCISE 12: USING THE COLON

In the spaces provided, rewrite the following sentences, inserting colons as needed. If a sentence is correct, mark it with a C.

EXAMPLE

After becoming rich I acquired three things I never had before friends, relatives, and lovers.

After becoming rich I acquired three things I never had

before: friends, relatives, and lovers.

1. The assignment for Bible as Literature is as follows John 21 17-30.

   _____

   _____

2. The town meeting broke up after a fiery outburst by one resident "Either clean up the streets or declare the neighborhood a hazard to the public's health!"

   _____

   _____

   _____

3. With a reputation for being overly chummy, President Reagan usually referred to his closest advisers as the "fellas" Edwin Meese, Michael Deaver, and Lyn Nofziger.

   _____

   _____

   _____

   _____

Use a colon to combine each group of sentences into a single sentence. You will have to revise wording and exclude some words to make the combined sentences read correctly.

EXAMPLE

Famous film director Alfred Hitchcock had several box-office hits. They were *Psycho*, *The Birds*, *Rear Window*, *North by Northwest*, and *Vertigo*.

Famous film director Alfred Hitchcock had several box-office hits: Psycho, The Birds, Rear Window, North by Northwest, and Vertigo.

4. Ernest Hemingway, a twentieth-century writer, wrote several novels. They are *The Sun Also Rises*, *Farewell to Arms*, *To Have and Have Not*, *For Whom the Bell Tolls*, *Across the River and into the Trees*, *The Old Man and the Sea*, and *Islands in the Stream*.

_____

_____

_____

_____

5. John stood on the hill and watched the sea. He saw swells forming on the horizon. He watched a school of dolphins breaking the surface. He studied the gulls wheeling and squawking over a bait boat.

_____

_____

_____

_____

EXERCISE 13: USING THE DASH

Rewrite the following sentences and insert dashes as needed.

EXAMPLE

His intention is clear: he is determined to become the world's top sprinter no matter what the cost.

His intention is clear: he is determined to become the

world's top sprinter — no matter what the cost.

1. There is no hope other than divine intervention that can stop nuclear missiles once they are launched.

   _____

   _____

   _____

2. The dangers of being a judge both real and threatened have increased in the last several years.

   _____

   _____

   _____

3. Bianchi, Klein, Guerciotti, Raleigh, Univega these are just a few of the bicycle brands from which cyclists can select.

   _____

   _____

   _____

4. "I cannot explain but somehow the night" she paused, her eyes turning helpless. "To tell the truth, it frightens me."

_____

_____

_____

5. Ralph Eggers a politician who has never lost an election announced his intention to run for Congress.

_____

_____

_____

Combine the following groups of sentences by using dashes. You will have to revise wording and exclude some words to make the combined sentences read correctly.

EXAMPLE

From running you can expect to experience aching feet and ankles, throbbing shins, and clicking knees. These are the physical joys that come from running on asphalt.

From running you can expect to experience aching

feet and ankles, throbbing shins, and clicking knees —

the physical joys that come from running on asphalt.

6. Jogging, swimming, racquetball, biking, and rowing are fine exercises. They all offer excellent workouts.

_____

_____

_____

7. The nation's economy is expanding, inflation is low, and the budget deficit is moving in the right direction. The budget deficit is still in triple digits.

_____

_____

_____

8. Day after day, the president watched the crisis grow. As the public opinion polls fell.

_____

_____

_____

9. Patrolman Swartz, like Dick Tracy, always gets his man. Dick Tracy is beloved by many children.

_____

_____

_____

Identify the author of the following quotation by using a dash so that the name stands separately from the text.

10. Iain Macleod once wrote, "History is too serious to be left to the historians."

_____

_____

_____

EXERCISE 14: USING QUOTATION MARKS

Supply quotation marks where they are needed and place other punctuation marks correctly in the following sentences. If a quotation should be set off in block form, place a *B* to indicate at which point the block would begin and an *E* to indicate where it would end. If a sentence is correct, mark it with a *C*.

EXAMPLE

The superintendent of schools claims: *B* By 1999 we will need 2,000 new teachers. We are worried because the latest surveys show that less than 5 percent of college students are training to be teachers. Unless we want double sessions and ill-prepared teachers we have to start planning for this situation right now. *E*

1. Did I hear that little bearded man say I want more gravy?

2. A cheery voice boomed over the blaring music Come in! Come in!

3. Mrs. Nelson stepped to the blackboard and wrote A Visit of Charity, The Hitch-hikers, and A Worn Path: titles of three outstanding stories by Eudora Welty.

4. The public information officer said that registration had increased 10 percent in the spring semester.

5. Robert Frost wrote Before I built a wall I'd ask to know / What I was walling in or walling out, / And to whom I was like to give offense. / Something there is that doesn't love a wall, / That wants it down.

6. Who is supposed to have said Don't fire until you see the whites of their eyes?

7. I'm so happy I could scream! she squealed.

8. Grandma's relief was evident: Look at that sign! Riverside—5 miles. We're almost home.

9. In 1927, Harry M. Warner of Warner Bros. said Who the hell wants to hear actors talk?

10. Did she really tell him to get lost?

11. One of my favorite Updike poems is Ex-Basketball Player.

12. One of Emily Dickinson's famous lines is I'm nobody! Who are you?

13. Cora was telling Bob that she had to do her chemistry homework tonight.

14. Do you remember what musical the line All the sounds of the earth are like music comes from?

15. He was fond of three quotations from H. L. Mencken: The men the American people admire most . . . are the most daring liars; No man ever went broke underestimating the taste of the American public; and The truth is, as everyone knows, that the great artists . . . are never puritans.

16. The teacher asked, Does anyone know who wrote The Destructors?

17. When he says Never! he means it.

18. Coleridge's famous poem begins In Xanadu did Kubla Khan / A stately pleasure-dome decree.

19. G. B. Shaw, an Irish dramatist, said Lack of money is the root of all evil.

20. Stephanie repeatedly asked to be allowed to go to Memphis by herself.

EXERCISE 15: USING PARENTHESES, BRACKETS, AND SLASHES

Add parentheses, brackets, and slashes as appropriate in the following sentences. Write added words, if any, as well as added punctuation along with adjacent words on the blank below each sentence.

EXAMPLE

The price of football tickets now ten dollars has been steadily rising.

tickets (now ten dollars) has

1. I can still hear my grandmother reciting "Hickory, Dickory, Dock. The mouse ran up the clock."

   _____

2. Hoover High with the longest winning record in the state is expected to win tonight's game.

   _____

3. We need to excel in all three phases of the campaign: 1 staff organization, 2 fundraising, and 3 issue-oriented publicity.

   _____

4. Lilly said, "I sure like to have vacation next week! You?"

   _____

5. The letter to the editor said, "I hate to say so, but you are all prejudice."

   _____

6. The John Muir footpath no longer in use winds all the way through the woods.

   _____

7. It's not an either or question! Find the middle ground.

   _____

8. "I'll never get tired of dancing she has been performing since she was six as long as people come to see me," she said.

_____

9. As they entered the hall decorated now for Christmas, they could hear the choir singing "Silent Night."

_____

10. His final plea was "Gimme a brake!"

_____

NAME _____   DATE_____

EXERCISE 16: USING END PUNCTUATION

Correct the following sentences by striking out and/or inserting periods, question marks, and exclamation points. If a sentence is correct, mark it with a C in the left-hand margin.

EXAMPLE

Pay attention, dunderhead!⫽

1. I did not believe the exam would be as easy as it was

2. Ms Nguyen always arrives right on time, but she leaves early.

3. Did you hear him ask what time it was??

4. That singer is my favorite T.V. performer.

5. When the weather cools off, let's go jogging (?) in the park.

6. I grabbed my boots, my raincoat, my umbrella, and my books and raced to the bus stop.

7. Be careful crossing the street.

8. My friends wanted to know if I was all right?

9. Do you think *King Henry and His Wives.* is a good title.

10. Our military science teacher was once a high officer in N.A.T.O..

11. I won't go. I won't go. I won't go.

12. When I graduate I plan to work for NBC or IBM.

13. Oh! Listen to that thunder!

14. I have an appointment with Dr Morgan today.

15. She's the one who wrote the poem "Who Am I?"

16. Do you believe in love at first sight?!?! Do you!!

17. Sit down!

18. Maria smiled (!) at me again today.

19. I want to know if you can operate a movie projector?

20. Many women prefer to be addressed as Ms. instead of as Miss or Mrs..

EXERCISE 1: USING CAPITALS

Rewrite each of the following items in the blanks provided, using capital letters wherever they are required. If an item is correct, write C in the blank.

EXAMPLE

main street   *Main Street* _____

1. robert r. smith, ph.d.   _____

2. twenty-fifth street   _____

3. the indian ocean   _____

4. the rocky mountains   _____

5. a famous russian dancer   _____

6. go south for three miles   _____

7. a french poodle   _____

8. president of the united states   _____

9. the romantic age   _____

10. the novel *for whom the bell tolls*   _____

11. the distant neptune   _____

12. university of southern california   _____

13. american bar association   _____

14. skippy peanut butter   _____

15. five college freshmen   _____

16. internal revenue service   _____

17. congressman jones   _____

18. Lincoln memorial _____

19. samir aziz, mba _____

20. "off and running: a day at the races" _____

21. winter term _____

22. hindus _____

23. oh my _____

24. o lord _____

25. sociology courses _____

NAME _____ DATE _____

EXERCISE 2: USING APOSTROPHES TO SHOW POSSESSION

Correct the use of apostrophes in the following sentences.

EXAMPLE

The governments attempts to scuttle rail transportation ignore the countrys need for a variety

of transportation services.

1. Mexicos tourist industry has been rocked by earthquakes.

2. His son-in-law and brother-in-laws business partnership still flourishes.

3. Joans friends will not play Parker Brothers Clue with her because she is so aggressive.

4. Cameron's, Rod's, and Allison's fish tank cracked last night.   JOINT POSSESSION

5. No matter what the circumstances, anyones tale of woe interests Zoe Ann.

6. *The Seasons of a Mans Life* discusses changes in mens psychological development.

7. The Mothers Crusade for peace begins its march in June.

8. Next summer I hope to visit the Peoples Republic of China.   People's

9. Without doubt, John and Charles's separate entries were similar.

10. Is this the companys final offer?

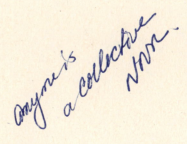

anyone is a collective noun

EXERCISE 3: USING APOSTROPHES TO SHOW POSSESSION

In each of the following items, the possessive relation is expressed by a phrase. Change each so that the possessive case is shown through the use of an apostrophe.

EXAMPLE

the bark of the dog

the dog's bark

1. songs of Benny Wright

   Benny Wright's songs   singular possession

2. films of Laurel and Hardy

   Laurel and Hardy's films   joint possession

3. rays of the sun

   the sun's rays

4. house of Nikki and Nikko

   Nikki and Nikko's house   joint possession

5. the power of the sergeant-at-arms

   the sergeant-at-arms' power   COMPOUND WORD
                                          Sing. possesion.

6. meeting of the ladies

   the ladies' meeting   plural possesion

7. temper of my sister-in-law

   my sister-in-law's temper   compound word

8. joy of the food servers

   the food servers' joy   plural possesion

9. temperament of the boys

the boys' temperment — plural possession

10. anger of the women

the women's anger — plural possession

EXERCISE 4: USING APOSTROPHES TO FORM CONTRACTIONS AND PLURALS

Correct any errors in apostrophe usage you find in the following sentences. You may have to insert apostrophes, delete apostrophes, or change the spelling of a word. To show a missing apostrophe, insert a caret (∨) where the apostrophe should go. Often the caret tip should be placed between two letters. To delete an unnecessary apostrophe, cross it out with a slash (/). If you need to correct a word's spelling, cross out the incorrect spelling and rewrite the correct one. If a sentence is correct, mark it with a C in the left-hand margin.

EXAMPLE

After the earthquake of 85 hit Mexico City, didn't the government prepare for the next one?

1. They're planning to bicycle from California to New York in '98.

2. The detective discovered who's *whose* fingerprint was on the doorknob.

C 3. Learning to multiply by tens is easy. *plurals ¿ Numbers .*

C 4. Growling and snapping, the dog chased its tail.

5. Instead of writing two 8s, he wrote two 3's. *plurals ¿ Numbers*

don't use contractions in theme's.

EXERCISE 5: USING ABBREVIATIONS

In the following sentences cross out and correct each abbreviation that is inappropriate or change a word or phrase to its abbreviated form if appropriate. If a sentence is correct, mark it with a C in the left-hand margin.

EXAMPLE

The Old Spaghetti Factory serves wonderful traditional Italian dishes (linguini with clam sauce,

ravioli, lasagna, ~~et cetera~~). *etc.*

1. Doctor Swartz studied Hemingway's novels for years.

2. Mrs. Thom. Kane disappeared from a Paris subway.

3. With a bow and arrow, he can hit a fly on a wall at twenty-five ft.

4. Dublin, Ire., still seems like a nineteenth-cen. city.

5. The Mustang skidded into the curve at eighty-five miles per hour.

6. The code was scribbled on pg. 111 in ch. 11.

7. Those in charge of the investigation (i.e., Dole and O'Neil) spent the night at the morgue.

8. Moscow, in Russia, has a pop. of 8,769,000.

9. He earns one hundred $ an hour.

10. The car pulled to a stop at No. 12 Downing Street.

11. The FBI investigates federal crimes committed within the borders of the USA.

12. John Monday lost the election because no one likes Mon.

13. In 1957 at Signal Hill, So. Cal., a flying saucer was sighted.

14. Prof. Robt. Casey teaches Psych. 100 on Tuesdays.

15. Mister Simon says, "There is no reward for the wicked—except in Las Vegas, Nev."

16. Aaron earned his J.D. degree at Southwestern University.

17. Harold & Maude are a couple of strange characters.

18. Union Copper paid $1,000,000 for the mineral rights.

19. May Fung, doctor of philosophy, is a specialist in psychoanalysis.

20. The Quality Environment Committee (QEC) plans to raise $100,000 in donations. Currently, QEC has collected $15,000.

EXERCISE 6: USING ITALICS

Edit the following sentences to correct errors in the use of italics. Underline any words, numbers, or letters that should be in italics. Circle any words, numbers, or letters that are underlined but should not be. If a sentence is correct, mark it with a C in the left-hand margin.

EXAMPLE

The title of Hemingway's <u>The Sun Also Rises</u> comes from (Ecclesiastes,) whereas the title of his <u>For Whom the Bell Tolls</u> comes from a John Donne meditation.

1. I have time either to watch Crossfire or to read Newsweek.

2. Picasso's mural Guernica dramatizes the bombing of a Basque town during the Spanish Civil War. It equals the emotional impact of Goya's painting The Third of May, 1808.

3. When first published, Arthur Janov's The Primal Scream was praised in the Chattanooga Times: "Sigmund Freud published the Interpretation of Dreams in 1900. Dr. Janov's work may be quite as important." Today the book cannot even be found on psychology department reading lists—c'est la vie.

4. The <u>Constitution</u> is the bedrock upon which our law is established.

5. In Absalom, Absalom, a novel set in the deep South, William Faulkner alluded to passages in the <u>Bible</u>, especially to passages in the <u>Old Testament</u>. In As I Lay Dying, an earlier novel, there are few biblical allusions.

6. Although Robert completed the exercises in Bold Strokes: A Guide to Beautiful Handwriting, he still makes his c's look like o's and his 7's look like 9's.

7. Lucas Samaras's <u>Rag Sculpture</u> is a single figure made of burlap and plaster; William King's <u>New People</u> is composed of nine figures made of vinyl.

8. The Silver Streak is the title of both a train and a film.

9. The bicycle chain was not just covered in grit—it was covered in true grit.

10. Typhoon is a Greek word that comes from the name of Typhon, a hundred-headed giant killed by Zeus.

11. Actor James Dean was killed in a car crash about forty years ago. Now the star of Rebel Without a Cause and Giant is a cult hero.

12. The plots of two novels, Raise the Titanic and The Dream of Eva Ryker, exploit the sinking of the world's largest luxury liner.

13. The early success of sputnik has been paled by contemporary efforts in space.

14. Many English words, such as hiss, pop, sizzle, buzz, and hum, imitate the sounds they represent.

15. The earth will be saved or destroyed by one creature—Homo sapiens.

16. The attorney read the Last Will and Testament of John Ramsey before the hushed relatives.

17. The word smog came from the first part of smoke and the second part of fog.

18. Brigitte ate the whole meal.

19. How are the l's pronounced in llama?

20. Head your papers by typing your name (first name first) in the upper-left-hand corner, type the course and number one line under your name, type the name of the professor on the next line, and type the date one line under that. Beneath that block, center and type the title of your paper. For example:

Harold Tobar

English 100

Professor Carroll

Oct. 30, 1996

Mystery in Sophocles's Oedipus Rex

NAME_____ DATE_____

EXERCISE 7: USING HYPHENS

In the following sentences, insert hyphens where they are needed. If the sentence is correct, mark it with a C in the left-hand margin. Consult your dictionary for accuracy.

EXAMPLE

Exboxers often end up as brain damaged victims unable to care for themselves.

1. The well made cabin has stood for one hundred and thirty five years.

2. American antiintellectualism peaked in the early 1950s.

3. The governor offered his plan for wallless prisons.

4. After one fourth of the audience walked out, the actors became discouraged.

5. The president elect is recuperating on Catalina Island.

6. Since Randy's parents will be traveling, his father and mother in law will host the Christmas dinner.

7. A hard nosed, mean eyed sergeant greeted the recruits.

8. Willy Loman believes that being well liked is the little known secret of success.

9. Bruce Catton books are notable for their dramatic recreation of the American Civil War.

10. Out of state vacationers do not understand the idiosyncratic driving patterns of southern Californians.

11. Push-ups will develop your biceps.

12. Pre World War I America seemed distant from world events.

13. The author, who is forty six, claims being creative has more to do with well developed goals than with a fired up intuition.

14. My great grandmother could read the tarot cards.

15. Phil Lambert, a hard driving entrepreneur, made his first million dollars at twenty five.

16. Six months after they signed the agreement, they were asked to resign the agreement during a public ceremony.

17. I inherited a toy that was my grandfather's childhood treasure—a hand painted jack in the box, which is at least two feet high.

18. Failure can often be attributed to the lack of selfconfidence and selfdiscipline.

19. Roberta was an allAmerican basketball star who also received straight A's.

20. Their devil take the hindmost attitude may lead to an I told you so catastrophe.

EXERCISE 8: USING NUMBERS

In the following sentences cross out any figures that should be spelled out and write the spelled-out numbers above them. Circle any spelled-out numbers that should be written in figures and write the figures above them. If a sentence is correct, mark it with a C in the left-hand margin.

EXAMPLE

twenty-six   *$4,925.*

At age ~~26,~~ my grandmother bought a beach house in 1929 for only ~~four thousand, nine hundred and twenty-five dollars.~~

1. 83 residents attended the city council meeting to stop construction of a two hundred and three foot footbridge.

2. New York's record high for July is one hundred and two degrees.

3. Although the demonstrators were peaceful, police arrested 95 and searched 200 more.

4. Since eighteen sixty-five, there have been seventeen assassinations and assassination attempts on prominent political figures in America.

5. How many players have batted better than .400 in a season?

6. The Irvine Senior Citizen Center celebrated the birthdays of 4 95-year-olds.

7. Although only twelve percent of newly commissioned army officers are West Point graduates, thirty-seven percent of all army generals wear West Point gray.

8. You will find the reference in chapter two, page forty-two, line seven.

9. The Los Angeles and New York play-off was a thriller—twenty-four to twenty-one, a field goal giving New York the edge.

10. Tune in at nine p.m. Eastern time to watch *Seinfeld*.

11. An *Advancement of Learning* (two hundred and twenty-five pages) is not a Federal Commission on Education report, but a well-conceived, well-executed detective novel.

12. Our national debt is approaching $three trillion.

13. Rancho Santa Margarita is a 5000-acre, master-planned community where fifty thousand people will live by the year two thousand and ten.

14. Sophocles died in four hundred and six B.C.; the world did not see such moving drama again until Shakespeare appeared almost 2 thousand years later.

15. In 1985, former Mafia capo Tommaso Buscetto accused 7 of 22 defendants of conspiring to import and sell $1.6 million worth of heroin in the United States.

16. The *Whydah*, discovered by treasure hunter Barry Clifford, is the 1st pirate ship ever found. Massachusetts will appropriate one-fourth of its $400 million treasure.

17. Biologists claim that as many as three thousand and fifty of twenty-two thousand species of higher plants native to the United States may become extinct.

18. Most copy machines print eight and one half × eleven inch copies, but this one will also print ten × fourteen inch copies.

19. July 4th is the day families get together to celebrate more than two hundred years of American democracy.

20. 2701 Fairview Road is a decaying mansion at the end of a 10-mile drive through a dense forest.

Answers

Part I: Grammar

Exercise 1: Identifying Nouns and Pronouns

1. Nouns: 2 servants, government
   Pronouns: 1 they
2. Nouns: 5 Ninjas, uniform, scarf, heads, eyes
   Pronouns: 1 their, their
3. Nouns: 3 night, shadows, enemy
   Pronouns 1 they
4. Nouns: 3 Ninja, combat, ninjutsu
   Pronouns: 0
5. Nouns: 3 blow, ninja, opponent
   Pronouns 0
6. Nouns: 5 warriors, use, weapons, stars, swords
   Pronouns: 0
7. Nouns: 4 ninjas, attacker, half, sword
   Pronouns: 1 they
8. Nouns: 3 ninjas, practices, enlightenment
   Pronouns: 1 them
9. Nouns: 5 service, government, mountains, Japan, fulfillment
   Pronouns: 1 they
10. Nouns: 7 arts, mysticism, ninjas, warriors, harmony, nature, civilization
    Pronouns 1 who
11. Nouns: 2 image, warriors
    Pronouns: 0
12. Nouns: 8 ninja, books, movies, superhero, young, way, Superman, parents
    Pronouns: 1 their
13. Nouns: 4 crusader, ninja, problems, police
    Pronouns: 0
14. Nouns: 7 boy, ninja, officer, nunchakus, sticks, chain, victim
    Pronouns: 1 which
15. Nouns: 7 Police, boy, part, gang, uniforms, money, children
    Pronouns: 0
16. Nouns: 6 incident, police, man, ninja, officers, sword
    Pronouns: 1 who
17. Nouns: 4 Psychologists, behavior, part, ninjas
    Pronouns: 2 those, who
18. Nouns: 5 People, characters, ninjas, identity, criminals
    Pronouns: 4 them, their, this, they
19. Nouns: 3 number, attacks, ninjas
    Pronouns: 0
20. Nouns: 5 ninja, media, ninja, government, enlightenment
    Pronouns: 1 who

Exercise 2: Identifying Verbs

1. is L
2. seems L
3. dedicate T
4. has T
5. pooled T
6. entered T
7. gleaned T
8. acquired T
9. collected T
10. made T
11. accumulated T
12. is L
13. may have changed H H T
14. deny T
15. is L
    did shift H T
16. knows I
    are becoming L
17. spent T
18. could exceed H T
19. will pay H T
20. will rise H I

Exercise 3 Identifying Adjectives and Adverbs

1. Adjectives: pot-bellied, tan, nimble, those
2. Adjectives: nuisance, dangerous
   Adverb: highly
3. Adjectives: deep, cautious
4. Adverbs: down, quickly
5. Adverbs: almost, always
6. Adverbs: unfortunately, sometimes
7. Adjective: mother
   Adverb: always
8. Adjective: bull
   Adverb: nearby
9. Adjective: all
10. Adjectives: nuisance, two
11. Adjectives: shark, cypress, large, beef smelly, old
    Adverb: very
12. Adjectives: some, beef, pungent
    Adverbs: Next, everywhere
13. Adjectives: patient, three
    Adverb: very
14. Adjective: smart
    Adverbs: fairly, not, before
15. Adjectives: his, his, hooked
    Adverbs: eventually, finally, quickly
16. Adjective: flat-bottom
    Adverb: Nightly
17. Adjective: hot
18. Adjectives: barbed, soft
19. Adverb: always
20. Adjectives: lumpy, white, Miami

Exercise 4: Identifying Prepositions, Conjunctions, and Interjections

1. Prepositions: 3 in, of, to
   Conjunctions: 0
   Interjections: 1 Oh no!
2. Prepositions: 5 of, of, to, to, of
   Conjunctions: 2 but, and
   Interjections: 0
3. Prepositions: 4 of, in, about, of
   Conjunctions: 1 but
   Interjections: 0
4. Prepositions: 4 of, from, from, of
   Conjunctions: 2 not only, but also
   Interjections: 0
5. Prepositions: 3 about, from, to
   Conjunctions: 2 and, and

Interjections: 0

6. Prepositions: 6 of, in, of, in, from, to
   Conjunctions: 1 and
   Interjections: 0

7. Prepositions: 2 of, by
   Conjunctions: 2 for, and
   Interjections: 0

8. Prepositions: 3 of, of, of
   Conjunctions: 3 and, when, and
   Interjections: 0

9. Prepositions: 4 in, of, in, of
   Conjunctions: 1 but
   Interjections: 0

10. Prepositions: 0
    Conjunctions: 0
    Interjections: How sad!

Exercise 5: Identifying Subjects and Predicates

1. Abalone divers and surfers
2. Paul Parsons, a skin diver
3. Tricia Kim, a surfer
4. Authorities
5. Sharks
6. That number
7. The center of the danger area
8. This ninety-mile stretch of coast and the Farallon Islands to the west
9. It
10. The assailants in every case
11. trace the shark attacks to recent animal protection rulings
12. make it illegal to hunt seals and otters
13. are staples in the great white's diet
14. lived and bred in the Red Triangle in 1961
15. flourished there just last year
16. has been increasing 3 percent a year

17. are responding to the increase in food supply by producing larger litters more rapidly
18. normally avoid humans but can mistake a diver in a black wet suit for a seal
19. Are . . . becoming a serious threat to California swimmers
20. are still fewer than deaths from lightning bolts or snakebites

Exercise 6: Identifying Complements

1. organism PN
2. insects, mammals, birds, diseases DO
3. crops DO
4. severe PA
5. battle DO
6. farmers IO; edge DO
7. drawbacks DO
8. potent PA
9. enemies DO
10. scientists IO; problem DO
11. None
12. threat PN
13. chain DO
14. crops DO
15. creatures DO; poisoned PA
16. chain DO; humans DO
17. real PA; work DO
18. them DO
19. simple PA; forms DO; destruction DO
20. difficult, challenging PA

Exercise 7: Using Prepositional Phrases
Individual student answers

Exercise 8: Using Appositives

Answers may vary

1. *TV Guide*, <u>the best-selling weekly magazine in the world</u>, publishes local television listings and articles about TV celebrities and shows.
2. Authorities claim that a nine-millimeter Ingram, <u>an automatic submachine gun</u>, is currently America's most dangerous street weapon.
3. *2001: A Space Odyssey*, <u>an early Stanley Kubrick success</u>, is still a popular cult film.
4. Scoop McLain, <u>a sarcastic and swaggering reporter</u>, stopped at Bernie's place last night.
5. Soap operas, <u>popular TV entertainment</u>, involve love, betrayal, success, and failure.
6. *Cosmopolitan*, <u>called *Cosmo* by its avid admirers</u>, is read by millions.
7. Weightlifting, <u>a popular sport among young men and women</u>, does very little for the cardiovascular system.
8. Coca-Cola, <u>still the largest selling soft drink</u>, has changed its flavor to compete more effectively with Pepsi-Cola.
9. Elvis Presley's death, <u>a shock to millions of fans</u>, came in 1977.
10. Richard Hollingshead, <u>a New Jersey businessman</u>, opened the world's first drive-in theater, <u>a massive parking lot equipped with movie screen and speakers in the stalls.</u>

Exercise 9: Using Prepositional Phrases and Appositives

Answers may vary.

1. Pope John Paul II visited the man who shot him, <u>Mehmet Ali Agca</u>, <u>in prison</u>.

2. The 1957 Chevrolet, <u>which came with large tail fins</u>, is popular with rare car collectors.
3. Axel Foley, <u>a Beverly Hills detective</u>, was arrested <u>for disturbing the peace</u>.
4. Bill Linn, <u>a spiritual medium who lives in New York</u>, predicted John F. Kennedy would be killed.
5. Belle Starr, <u>a notorious outlaw</u>, was shot <u>to death</u> <u>in Oklahoma</u> when she was forty-one years old.
6. Eric Fischl, <u>a forty-three-year-old artist</u>, portrays the anxiety he sees and experiences <u>in American life</u>.
7. The tango, <u>a dance that began a century ago in Buenos Aires bordellos</u>, is once again becoming popular in <u>New York</u> nightspots.
8. Logic bombs, <u>bits of destructive software coding designed to confuse a computer system</u>, are exploding every week <u>in the country's leading business firms</u>.
9. <u>In its May 20, 1985</u>, issue, *Time* magazine quoted John Dryden, <u>an English poet and critic</u>: "Forgiveness <u>to the injured</u> doth belong."
10. Mary Harris, <u>a native of Cork, Ireland</u>, organized labor unions <u>in West Virginia, Pennsylvania, and Colorado</u>.

Exercise 10: Identifying Infinitive and Participle Phrases

1. to be the moment the sun reached its zenith INF
2. traumatized by stiff competition PART
3. holding a phone receiver in each hand PART
   to place stock orders INF

4. Discouraged by time's power PART
5. to organize INF to traumatize our lives INF
6. The atomic clock is a perfect machine to pace our lives precisely.
7. Precise timekeeping is necessary to aid submarine navigation, oil exploration, and television transmission.
8. The Navy sends a 150-pound atomic clock named Mr. Clock to other countries for technicians to use in the adjustment of other timekeeping systems.
9. The timekeepers at the Naval Observatory have one main duty: to keep precise time for a system of navigation satellites.
10 Navigation satellites, to be positioned precisely in the sky, will soon monitor world time, permitting official time to be beamed to clocks everywhere.
11-15. Individual student answers.

Exercise 11: Using Gerunds and Participles
Individual student answers

Exercise 12: Writing Absolute Phrases
1. The restaurant closed for the night, the street seemed strangely empty
2. The election over, the votes remained to be counted and the winners to be announced.
3. The rod bending like a whip, its tip vibrating like a snake's tongue, Tina stood on the riverbank and reeled in the trout.
4. The wind whipped over the roof of the abandoned building, a soft rumble echoing through the empty room.
5. The tile growing wet from the stream, Ian felt the slick floor beneath his bare feet.

Exercise 13: Identifying Clauses
1. D
2. D
3. M
4. N
5. D
6. which means full of anxiety, frustration, and stress ADJ
7. which is a disease ADJ
   that affects blood sugar levels ADJ
8. who are successful ADJ
   because these heroes make money at the box office ADV
9. if you believe films affect behavior ADV
10. who believes displaced aggression is increasing ADJ
    when a solid 25 percent of the population is capable of committing random violence ADV
11. If you expect sociopaths to be ruthless killers, you are wrong because many of them are professionals such as lawyers, doctors, and bankers.
12. Ten percent of the population, which includes drug abusers, juvenile delinquents, and people with explosive behavior, may be antisocial.
13. Antisocial behavior will become more common because drug abuse and violent behavior is increasing among ten- to thirteen-year-olds.
14. As children grow up with little parental concern or supervision, society becomes the victim.

15. Many people who are the most fearful of sudden attack handle the threat by enrolling in self-defense classes or by arming themselves.

16. Many people with explosive personality disorders, after realizing they get into too much trouble chasing strangers or brandishing crowbars in parking lots, eventually confine their outbursts to their homes.

17. Some people have built-in cultural values that might inhibit aggressive displays toward family members, while others show aggression to family members that they would not show to friends.

18. When violence erupts outside the family, the victims are often employees of large companies or government agencies that deal with the public.

19. Many companies and agencies that have thousands of complaints weekly do not want to completely satisfy complaining clients.

20. As an aggressive client becomes angry, the employee who listens to the complaint becomes the target.

Part II: Sentence Errors

Exercise 1: Correcting Sentence Fragments
Answers may vary.

1. Because Chinese scholars have been so careful to record details over so many centuries, we have more interesting information about Chinese dragons than dragons of other cultures.
2. Most dragons, for example, laid their eggs near rivers, while a few preferred hillsides.
3. The hatching of a dragon egg had an impressive effect on the weather, causing the wind to increase if the newborn were male and almost cease if it were female.
4. C
5. In the dragon literature of China, great emphasis was placed on the number of scales and claws a dragon possessed.
6. Some scholars argued that a real dragon had exactly eighty-one scales, a figure obtained by squaring the masculine number nine.
7. Others believed that dragons were both masculine and feminine and added thirty-six scales to include the feminine number six squared.
8. The most powerful dragons were the five-clawed variety. They could be shown on decorations for the imperial house only.
9. According to one early authority cited by the Shuo Wen dictionary, dragons had the power to be visible or invisible at will.
10. They also had the ability to change size from a tiny being the size of a silkworm to an enormous presence filling the space between heaven and earth
11. Transformations, too, were tricks dragons used, making it difficult for people to study their behavior.
12. To get a good look at a dragon, a person had to approach it at the right time, when it was asleep or thinking angry or lustful thoughts.
13. C
14. One dragon, in female human form, is said to have joined the court of the emperor to satisfy her desire to devour men.
15. A Han dynasty emperor, who supposedly caught a dragon while fishing, had it served as a dinner dish, a delicacy of blue bones and purple flesh.
16. The bones and teeth of dragons ground into powder served as medicine which cured a variety of ailments, including fevers, gallstones, ulcers, paralysis, and boils.
17. C
18. Doctors also recommended dragon brains, liver, skin, and fat as powerful curative agents.
19. Collecting dragon saliva, a substance which was valued as a perfume, often took years of patient waiting to make sure the dragon had left his home and the saliva could be gathered safely.
20. Nowadays, although some belief in dragons still persists, their chief function is the symbolic decorations of manufactured items.

Exercise 2: Correcting Sentence Fragments
Answers may vary.

1. Hercules, possibly the greatest Greek

hero, began his dragon killing early, strangling two snakes just months after he was born.

2. As he grew to manhood, he traveled throughout the Mediterranean area and performed many feats of strength and daring.

3. The priestess of Apollo told Hercules he could become immortal as soon as he performed the labors assigned to him by Eurystheus.

4. One of the labors was to kill the Hydra, a water monster that lived in the swamps of Lerna.

5. C

6. Because its breath was poisonous and even the smell of its tracks could kill, it was impossible for Hercules to subdue it unless he held his breath for the entire fight.

7. To complicate matters further, whenever Hercules struck off one of the Hydra's heads, two or three grew in its place.

8. Hercules finally killed the Hydra with the help of a friend who set fire to a forest and burned each stump, preventing new growth.

9. Another notable dragon killer was Perseus, the son of the god Zeus and a beautiful but mortal woman, Danaë.

10. Returning from his major triumph, the slaying of Medusa, Perseus heard that a certain King Cepheus had been forced to chain his beautiful daughter to a rock as an offering to a dragon who had been ravaging his land.

11. Perseus fell in love with the beautiful daughter, Andromeda, and promised the king to rescue her if he could marry her.

12. Because he had the help of a cap that made him invisible and a pair of winged sandals, Perseus apparently killed the dragon with ease.

13. Arrangements were made for the wedding of Perseus and Andromeda over the objections of Phineus, another suitor for Andromeda's hand.

14. Fortunately, Perseus had another valuable weapon with him that he had saved from an earlier adventure.

15. This weapon was the head of Medusa. It had the power to turn anyone who looked at it to stone, and Perseus always carried it with him in a wallet draped over his shoulder.

16. As Phineus attacked Perseus, Perseus showed Medusa's head, and the wedding continued without further interruption.

17. C.

18. While attempting to rescue his sister from the hands of Zeus, he came upon a ferocious dragon guarding the only available source of water.

19. After slaying the dragon, Cadmus sowed its teeth in the ground on the advice of Athena. From the buried teeth sprang a whole army of soldiers.

20. To prevent them from attacking him, Cadmus cleverly threw rocks among the soldiers, making each think he had been attacked by another.

Exercise 3: Correcting Comma Splices and Fused Sentences

Answers may vary.

1. C
2. CS He completed an amazing number of

works in a short life; he died at age thirty-five.

3. FS Mozart was born in Salzburg, Austria, in 1756. His first performing tour was only six years later in 1762.

4. FS His father was a violinist, composer, and teacher, and his sister was an accomplished pianist.

5. CS The young Mozart traveled, on tour, to Italy, France, and England. The rulers of each country greeted him as a child genius.

6. CS In Italy he was decorated by the pope; in England he wrote his first symphony.

7. C

8. FS Now a mature musician, Mozart served as concertmaster in a Salzburg orchestra on and off for ten years. When he was in his mid-twenties, he won a commission to write an opera for a Munich carnival.

9. CS Opera was Mozart's favorite musical form; the piano was his favorite instrument.

10. FS *Don Giovanni* is considered by most critics to be his best opera. His technique of using the orchestra to carry some of the emotion of the story was ahead of its time.

11. C

12. FS The following year he wrote three of his best string quartets. These were commissioned by the King of Prussia.

13. FS Mozart never seemed to lack commissions; almost everything he composed was done on assignment for someone else.

14. FS One nobleman asked Mozart to compose a requiem mass in secret because he wanted to have the work performed as his own.

15. In spite of his great number of works and the acclaim they brought him, he was a poor man. When he died in 1791, he was buried in an unmarked grave.

Exercise 4: Correcting Comma Splices and Fused Sentences

Diego Rivera, Mexico's famous revolutionary artist, created controversy throughout his life. His giant murals celebrating the cause of the working class were too radical for many people. A portrait of Lenin appeared in a mural he was painting at Rockefeller Center in New York City. In spite of a public outcry, he refused to remove it though he did offer to add a portrait of Abraham Lincoln. That wasn't enough. His commission was canceled. The unfinished mural was destroyed. He had lost this battle; however, he later challenged all the artistic *isms* of the early twentieth century. He disdained ordinary canvas-sized pictures because he believed that they inevitably end up in stuffy museums or the homes of the rich. Instead, he looked for huge walls on buildings where art could be used as a weapon in the class struggle. A typical Rivera mural is ablaze with color and full of people; it condemns exploitation of the masses or symbolizes the strength of purpose of awakened workers. Out of his sympathy for the poor, Rivera joined the Communist Party, but he denounced the part in 1929; then he was attacked by both leftists and rightists. He often carried a pistol for protection. When he died in 1957, controversy surrounded his funeral, too. The Communist Party covered his coffin with a red flag. Others opposed this gesture; fights erupted on the streets even as his body was lowered into the grave.

Exercise 5: Correcting Errors in Subject and Verb Agreement

1. is
2. come
3. is
4. C
5. is
6. knows
7. exists
8. are
9. is
10. is
11. loves
12. is
13. was
14. is
15. C
16. C
17. are
18. have
19. relaxes
20. was

Exercise 6: Selecting Correct Pronouns For Pronoun and Antecedent Agreement

1. who
2. their
3. his or her
4. their
5. theirs
6. its
7. his
8. who
9. that
10. who
11. it
12. its
13. its
14. its
15. her
16. his or her
17. its
18. their
19. his or her
20. that, its

Exercise 7: Selecting Correct Pronoun Case

1. She
2. her, me
3. His
4. him
5. Whoever
6. we
7. them
8. We
9. whoever
10. Whom
11. whom, us
12. I
13. Who
14. I
15. your
16. His
17. Who
18. they
19. him, her
20. her, me

Exercise 8: Selecting Correct Verb Forms and Learning Principal Parts of Verbs

1. did   (do, did, done)
2. found   (find, found, found)
3. heard   (hear, heard, heard)
4. paid   (pay, paid, paid)
5. brought   (bring, brought, brought)
6. wore   (wear, wore, worn)
7. fell   (fall, fell, fallen)
8. hidden   (hide, hid, hidden)
9. given   (give, gave, given)
10. forbidden   (forbid, forbade or forbad, forbidden)
11. ran   (run, ran, run)
12. torn   (tear, tore, torn)
13. begun   (begin, began, begun)
14. slid   (slide, slid, slid or slidden)
15. caught   (catch, caught, caught)
16. cut   (cut, cut, cut)
17. saw   (see, saw, seen)
18. flew   (fly, flew, flown)
19. stung   (sting, stung, stung)
20. written   (write, wrote, written)

Exercise 9: Changing Verb Tenses

Part A

Of course, we all enjoyed the excitement of being in a crowd, and this reaction could not be ignored. But there were crowds and crowds. It was pleasant enough to be in a "spectator crowd," but not so appealing to find yourself in the middle of a rush-hour crush. The difference between the two was that the spectator crowd was all facing in the same direction and concentrating on a distant point of interest. Attending a theatre, there were twinges of rising hostility toward the stranger who sat down immediately in front of you or the one who squeezed into the seat next to you. The shared armrest could become a polite, but distinct, territorial boundary-dispute region. However, as soon as the show began, these invasions of Personal Space were forgotten and the attention was focused beyond the small space where the crowding was taking place. Then, each member of the audience felt himself spatially related, not to his cramped neighbors, but to the actor on the stage, and the distance was, if anything, too great. In the rush-hour crowd, by contrast, each member of the pushing throng was competing with his neighbors all the time. There was no escape to a spatial relation with a distant actor, only the pushing, shoving bodies all around.

Part B

The program will be easy to use even without the tutorial. The main menu will remain at the top of your screen at all times. You will access seven pop-up submenus by hitting the Esc or slash (/) keys. Once in a submenu, the program will provide step-by-step instructions at the bottom of your screen, prompting you through each menu operation. The Range menu will allow you to create rectangles and patterns, while Box commands will be for drawing rectangles with thick, thin, dotted, or double-line borders. The Ext commands will permit enlarging, stretching, underlining, and boldfacing, and Edit will allow you to undo a command or create a backup file. File will include all file maintenance operations.

Print will control all printing operations including condensed type and multiple copies. Quit will require you to confirm your intention to leave the program.

Exercise 10: Selecting Correct Tenses in Sequence

1. will be
2. had won
3. loaded
4. was
5. believe
6. have finished
7. wants
8. has been
9. had been
10. is

Exercise 11: Using Active and Passive Voice

Part A

1. Emphasizes receiver of the action: the warehouse.
2. Doer of the action is unknown.
3. Emphasizes receiver of the action: a woman.
4. Emphasizes the action itself: was rushed.
5. Doer of the action is unknown.

Part B

6. Inexperienced mechanics did the repairs on my automobile.
7. The architect submitted a detailed rendering.
8. I wrote the essay.
9. A
10. Halley's comet disappointed many stargazers.

11. The executive committee approved the new guidelines.
12. The doctor removed a small chip of wood from his eye.
13. A
14. A
15. Do you know if the Ski Club is going to serve the dinner?
16. When the cleanup crew arrived, litter covered the picnic grounds.
17. A
18. Kim's home movie won the first-place trophy.
19. Gary Richards' last minute desperation shot won the game.
20. A.

Exercise 12: Using Adjectives and Adverbs

1. popular   adjective   activity
2. Unfortunately   adverb   can (not) be located
3. cautiously   adverb   estimates
4. well   adverb   mean
   permanent   adjective   record
5. unintentionally   adverb   dug up
6. considerable   adjective   difficulty
7. specifically   adverb   for the capsule
8. earlier   adjective   time
9. funniest   adjective   case
10. loudly   adverb   insisted
11. largest   adjective   capsule
12. most expensive   adjective   capsule
13. worst   adjective   record
14. better   adjective   material
15. Specially   adverb   designed
    safely   adverb   survive

16. surely adverb will keep
17. recently adverb suggested
    concentrated adjective effort
18. seriously adverb thought
19. uneasy (predicate) adjective people
20. perfectly adverb happy

Part III: Sentence Clarity and Variety

Exercise 1: Using Coordination and Subordination

Answers may vary.

1. When she rides a bicycle, Shirley comes home from school fifteen minutes before James.
2. If you read the newspaper, you will learn about politics.
3. Max wanted to learn French, so he went to Paris.
4. One of my aunts, who teaches psychology, lives in San Francisco.
5. The police chief was suspicious when he smelled a strong odor coming from beneath his house.
6. She moved to another part of the city so she would be closer to her work.
7. Bobby Joe was cooking dinner when the phone rang.
8. Yung was tired because he had been looking all over town for his dog.
9. Whenever I turn on the television, I see a commercial first.
10. If you are going to the grocery store, buy me some gum.

Exercise 2: Correcting Excessive Coordination and Subordination

Answers may vary.

1. Our dog ran away, and the cat that lived next door disappeared. Some of the neighbors believe that there is a connection.
2. No one has seen the dog and cat for three days, yet Mr. Withers and Ms. Conrad insist that the dog and cat will both return.
3. Mr. Withers works in the local furrier's, and Ms. Conrad works in the local pet food factory. Both of them drive to work in the same car because they want to save money.
4. After Ms. Conrad arrives at the pet food factory, she begins her day by turning on the photocopy machine and her computer.
5. Mr. Withers begins his day at the furrier's by brushing six or seven fur coats so that they will be fluffy.
6. These furs are expensive, though they are made from an acrylic and polyester combination that makes them look like real fur.
7. Many of our nearby neighbors have organized a nightly search party for our missing dog and cat.
8. The cat, Butch, and the dog, Mimi, have never been good friends. No one believes that they suddenly decided to leave like pets leave in television cartoons.
9. Pets are enjoyable, but when you realize how much time it takes to care for a pet properly, sometimes you lose interest in their welfare.
10. Calvin's old dog lies around the house all day, and his pet snake silently slides through the house nightly. His pet hamster, though, exercises happily in his cage, unaware of the dangers just beyond his wire enclosure.

Exercise 3: Placing Modifiers

Answers may vary.

1. Once an assistant in many heart operations and now a world-famous heart surgeon in his own right, Denton Cooley estimates that he has performed at least 65,000 heart operations.
2. He has one of the lowest mortality rates of any heart surgeon.
3. He has performed nearly ninety-one heart transplants.
4. Dr. Cooley also developed and implanted the first temporary heart.
5. Among a number of adventures and richly deserved awards, his career includes doing the first heart operation.
6. In the mid-1950s, he invented one of the early heart-lung machines.
7. He has amassed a personal fortune in excess of $20 million.
8. In early December 1967, Cooley heard on the radio that Dr. Christiaan Barnard had done the first human heart transplant.
9. Like most surgeons, Cooley was dumfounded.
10. Dr. Barnard's courage stimulated Cooley.

Exercise 4: Correcting Faulty Pronoun Reference

Answers may vary.

1. It is necessary that we build a new foundation for our statue of General Martinet. The old foundation is crumbling.
2. The statue has stood in the park for more than fifty years. The park is crowded every Fourth of July.
3. The police should have arrested the people who poked holes in the statue's weak foundation.
4. The statute looks as if it will collapse any minute.
5. If the statue falls and pieces of it fly through the air, some nearby people may be hurt.
6. The city council invited citizens to help rebuild the statue.
7. Time is passing, and no one is doing anything about the statue.
8. If the foundation is not replaced before the next Fourth of July, it may not be a happy celebration because the statue may collapse.
9. If General Martinet's statue collapses, people will have no reason to visit the park.
10. The statue's collapse could happen because nobody seems too interested.

Exercise 5: Correcting Faulty Shifts

Answers may vary.

1. Sixty percent of a newly-designed engine is made of plastic.
2. Plastic makes the engine lighter.
3. A child could easily pull a child's wagon loaded with the engine.
4. A child would feel proud to pull a wagon loaded with the powerful engine.
5. The new engine is called the Polimotor. It was designed by Matthew Holtzberg.
6. At a recent engineer's meeting, Holtzberg calmly revealed that most of the engine's moving parts are made of Torlon, a heat-resistant plastic resin.
7. The engine block itself is made of graphite-fabric and epoxy composite.

8. In the future, drivers will have fewer mechanical problems because of their Polimotors

9. According to Holtzberg, the first question people ask when they see a plastic engine is, "Why doesn't this thing melt?"

10. Holtzberg explains that the engineers put metal where the greatest heat is generated.

Exercise 6: Making Sentences Logically Complete

Answers may vary.

1. Our car is seventeen years old.
2. When our car was new, it averaged thirty miles per gallon; now it averages twenty.
3. We would trade in our car, except for the expense of four years of monthly payments.
4. No new-car dealer will take our old clunker for a down payment. Our down payment will have to be cash.
5. We went to the Ford Dealer, then to the Chevrolet dealer.
6. Both dealers said our car is too old.
7. Our town has more old cars than any other town in the country.
8. Compared with some old cars, ours is not so bad.
9. Our car looks old and ugly compared with new cars.
10. Someday, our car won't get us to our destination.

Exercise 7: Correcting Faulty Parallelism

1. Athletes develop exceptional muscle tone, unusual lung capacity, and healthy mental attitudes.

2. Coaches aid athletes by helping them both physically and emotionally.
3. Aerobics helps the lungs, the heart, and the muscles.
4. Many athletes train by doing aerobic exercises and lifting weights.
5. Aerobic training builds endurance, and weight training builds muscles.
6. Second-rate athletes are often found standing on the sidelines or warming the bench.
7. Some athletes refuse to exercise, but they want playing time.
8. Occasionally, coaches do not know whether to permit an athlete to play or to require the athlete to practice more.
9. All coaches like to see their athletes play hard, win often, and enjoy a successful season.
10. After a particularly rough game, many athletes enjoy going to a party, relaxing among friends, or staying home to watch a late-night movie on television.

Exercise 8: Identifying Sentence Structures and Forms

1. complex
2. loose
3. loose
4. simple
5. loose
6. loose
7. periodic
8. compound
9. periodic
10. simple

11. loose
12. complex
13. loose
14. complex
15. compound

16. compound
17. loose
18. periodic
19. balanced
20. loose

Part IV: Punctuation

Exercise 1: Using Commas with Coordinating Conjunctions Linking Main Clauses

1. uttered, yet
2. word, and
3. 1706, and
4. *am not*, so
5. Atlantic, but
6. used, but
7. *am not*, yet
8. use, for
9. anymore, yet
10. smirk, and

Exercise 2: Using Commas with Introductory Phrases and Clauses

1. past, dangerous
2. women, men
3. stunts, there
4. resistance, stunt
5. 5-foot-3, with; frame, Simone Boisserer
6. ballerina, she
7. C
8. floor, she
9. cleared, she
10. like, she

Exercise 3: Writing Sentences with Introductory Phrases

Individual student answers.

Exercise 4: Using Commas To Set Off Nonrestrictive Elements

1. poets, like wandering troubadours, would
2. C (that has a central nervous system)
3. C (throughout the United States)
4. George Raft, both of whom began their careers as dancers, became
5. week, which
6. C (who has time and patience)
7. C (*The Crying of Lot 49*)
8. Fabian, whose full name is Fabian Anthony Forte, was
9. army, traveling under the cover of darkness, arrived
10. advocates, who came from every segment of American society, marched; disarmament, a goal millions of ordinary citizens are still working to achieve.

Exercise 5: Combining Sentences

1. Having gathered at the palace gates, the crowd listened to the voice coming over the loudspeaker.
2. The senior class that was the rowdiest in the school's history purchased a new scoreboard for the school.
3. The go-away bird, the gray loerie, gets its nickname from a call that sounds human.
4. Sitting in the back row, the old man collapsed when the race started.
5. Holographic images, which are created by laser beams, appear to be three-dimensional.

6. Western Samoa, where my mother was born, has 160,000 inhabitants.

7. Striking in the first century B. C., the invading Roman legions brought Britain into contact with the Continent.

8. At their Morocco meeting, Winston Churchill and Franklin Roosevelt agreed to force Adolf Hitler to surrender unconditionally.

9. After the central character, John Blackthorne, is shipwrecked in feudal Japan, he survives a grueling incarceration.

10. Stephen Crane, who had never been a soldier, wrote *The Red Badge of Courage*, a novel about a soldier in the American Civil War.

Exercise 6: Using Commas To Set Off Parenthetical Expressions and Mild Interjections

1. moreover, the

2. vampires, for example, leave; furthermore, they

3. Of course, as you well know, vampires; and, according to tradition, a vampire

4. Yes, garlic;   cross, to most people's surprise, doesn't

5. however, a

6. agree, however, that

7. C

8. fact, novelist;   prince, unfortunately, was

9. C

10. not, but;   otherwise, life

Exercise 7: Using Commas in a Series and Between Coordinate Adjectives

1. food, clothing, and services.

2. poorly housed, poorly dressed, poorly fed.

3. hungry, uneducated immigrants

4. arrived in New York, soon moved north to Boston and south to Philadelphia, and then trekked west toward California.

5. far-sighted, courageous leaders;   towns, lakes, and rivers

6. 120-foot, 12-second, historic ride.

7. quit their jobs, abandoned their families, and ignored their common-sense

8. catfish, bald eagle, rattlesnake, and hummingbird;   whiskers like a cat, a head of white feathers, a rattle like a child's toy, and wings that hum in flight.

9. bank closings, bankruptcies, factory shutdowns, and farm and home mortgage foreclosures

10. C

Exercise 8: Using Commas To Set Off Contrasting Expressions, Interrogative Elements, and Explanatory Words Used with Direct Quotations

1. "Americans," reports one health expert, "have always associated an affluent lifestyle with a diet heavy in fat and sugar."

2. "Mix fat and sugar with large quantities of salt and the diet will kill you," one nutritionist claims.

3. Commercial meat, an American diet staple, is highly suspect, not just because of the fat and cholesterol.

4. Whenever you bite into a hamburger or leg of lamb, along with the seasoning you are probably getting generous helpings of everything from growth hormones, not for your growth but for the animal's, to printer's ink from paper recycled into feed for fiber.

5. Not an appetizing thought, is it?

6. One rancher actually asked, "Why should city folk worry about chemicals in their meat?" He continued, "They use chemical sanitizers, insecticides, and tranquilizers, don't they?"

7. C

8. "Chemicals are becoming so widely used in cattle raising that consumers might soon need a prescription to buy a hamburger," one critic joked.

9. Chemicals, not just the high cost of meat, are one reason health-conscious people are turning to fish.

10. The sushi bar, in contrast to the steak house, is the latest success story in American dining.

Exercise 9: Comma Review 1

1. 1970s,
2. Sometimes, though, however,
3. First,
4. businesslike, notes, recipient,
5. Second, unsuccessful,
6. addition,
7. C
8. item, problem, documents,
9. period, weeks,
10. weeks,
11. C
12. days,   phone, of course)
13. Now, phone, maintenance, abuse,
14. claims, problems, thinking, avoided,"
15. sense," adds,
16. not, instance, telephone, assembly,
17. numbers,
18. fall, dial,
19. all, telephone,
20. maintenance,

Exercise 10: Comma Review 2

1. Cats," tale,
2. father, farmer,
3. acolyte (no comma)
4. things,
5. hours,
6. C
7. right, moreover, more,
8. study, draw, wise, stern, said, temple!" (no comma) places", warned, finger,
9. C
10. more,
11. sorrowful, temple,
12. home, priest,
13. But, unfortunately, closed (no comma) goblin,
14. temple, entered,
15. C
16. acolyte," himself,
17. him, however, screens,
18. tired, box, ink,
19. screens, tired,
20. screens, words,
21. large, why,
22. temple,
23. one, screen, in,

24. night,
25. instead, still,
26. C
27. Finally,
28. First, Next, saw, it, rat,
29. Suddenly,
30. Later, artist

Exercise 11: Using Semicolons

1. diets; (delete comma)
2. drinking; (delete comma)
3. wrote; (delete comma)
4. (delete semicolon)
5. day, (delete semicolon)
6. alert; (delete comma)   sleep; (delete comma)
7. withdrawal, (delete semicolon)
8. schedules; (delete comma)
9. breaks; (delete comma) coffee,
10. C

Exercise 12: Using the colon

1. The assignment for Bible as Literature is as follows: John 21: 17-30.
2. The town meeting broke up after a fiery outburst by one resident: "Either clean up the streets or declare the neighborhood a hazard to the public's health!"
3. With a reputation for being overly chummy, President Reagan usually referred to his closest advisers as the "fellas": Edwin Meese, Michael Deaver, and Lyn Nofziger.
4. Ernest Hemingway, a twentieth-century writer, wrote several novels: *The Sun Also Rises, Farewell to Arms, To Have and Have Not, For Whom the Bell Tolls, Across the River and into the Trees, The Old Man and the Sea,* and *Islands in the Stream.*
5. John stood on the hill and watched the sea: swells forming on the horizon, a school of dolphins breaking the surface, and gulls wheeling and squawking over a bait boat.

Exercise 13: Using the Dash

1. There is no hope—other than divine intervention—that can stop nuclear missiles once they are launched.
2. The dangers of being a judge—both real and threatened—have increased in the last several years.
3. Bianchi, Klein, Guerciotti, Raleigh, Univega—these are just a few of the bicycle brands from which cyclists can select.
4. "I cannot explain but somehow the night"—she paused, her eyes turning helpless. "To tell the truth, it frightens me."
5. Ralph Eggers—a politician who has never lost an election—announced his intention to run for Congress.
6. Jogging, swimming, racquetball, biking, and rowing—all these offer excellent workouts.
7. The nation's economy is expanding, inflation is low, and the budget deficit—still in triple digits—is moving in the right direction.
8. Day after day, the president watched the crisis grow—as the public opinion polls fell.
9. Patrolman Swartz, like Dick Tracy—beloved by many children—always gets his man.

10 "History is too serious to be left to the historians,"

—Iain Macleod

Exercise 14. Using Quotation Marks

1. Did I hear the little bearded man say, "I want more gravy"?
2. A cheery voice boomed over the blaring music: "Come in! Come in!"
3. Mrs. Nelson stepped to the blackboard and wrote, "A Visit of Charity," "The Hitch-hikers," and "A Worn Path," titles of three outstanding stories by Eudora Welty.
4. C
5. Robert Frost wrote (B) Before I built a wall I'd ask to know/ What I was walling in or walling out,/ And to whom I was like to give offense./ Something there is that doesn't love a wall,/ That wants it down.(E)
6. Who is supposed to have said, "Don't fire until you see the whites of their eyes"?
7. "I'm so happy I could scream!" she squealed.
8. Grandma's relief was evident: "Look at the sign! 'Riverside—5 miles.' We're almost home."
9. In 1927, Harry M. Warner of Warner Bros. said, "Who the hell wants to hear actors talk?"
10. C
11. One of my favorite Updike poems is "Ex-Basketball Player."
12. One of Emily Dickinson's famous lines is "I'm nobody! Who are you?"
13. C
14. Do you remember what musical the line "All the sounds of the earth are like music" comes from?
15. He was fond of three quotations from H.L. Mencken: "The men the American people admire most . . . are the most daring liars"; "No man ever went broke underestimating the taste of the American public"; and "The truth is, as everyone knows, that the great artists . . . are never puritans."
16. The teacher asked, "Does anyone know who wrote 'The Destructors'?"
17. When he says "Never!" he means it.
18. Coleridge's famous poem begins "In Xanadu did Kubla Khan/ A stately pleasure-dome decree."
19. G. B. Shaw, an Irish dramatist, said, "Lack of money is the root of all evil."
20. C

Exercise 15: Using Parentheses, Brackets, and Slashes

1. Dock./ The mouse
2. Hoover High—with the longest winning record in the state—is expected to win tonight's game.
3. (1) (2) (3)
4. "I sure [would] like. . . [Would] you?"
5. prejudice[d]."
6. footpath (no longer in use) winds
7. either/or
8. dancing—she has been performing since she was six— as long
9. hall (decorated now for Christmas), they
10. "Gimme a brake [sic]!"

Exercise 16: Using End Punctuation

1. Was.
2. Ms.
3. was? (Delete one question mark)
4. TV (Delete periods)
5. jogging in the park (Delete question mark and parentheses)
6. C
7. C (or street!)
8. right. (Delete question mark)
9. title? (Change period to question mark)
10. NATO (Delete periods)
11. go! go! go! (Change periods to exclamation points)
12. graduate,
13. C
14. Dr.
15. C
16. sight? you! (Delete other exclamation points and a question mark)
17. C
18. smiled at me (Delete exclamation point and parentheses)
19. projector. (Change question mark to period)
20. Mrs. (Delete one period)

Part V: Mechanics

Exercise 1:Using Capitals
1. Robert R. Smith, Ph.D.
2. Twenty-fifth Street
3. the Indian Ocean
4. the Rocky Mountains
5. a famous Russian dancer
6. Go south for three miles.
7. a French poodle
8. President of the United States
9. the Romantic Age
10. the novel *For Whom the Bell Tolls*
11. the distant Neptune
12. University of Southern California
13. American Bar Association
14. Skippy peanut butter
15. five college freshmen
16. Internal Revenue Service
17. congressman Jones
18. Lincoln Memorial
19. Samir Aziz, MBA
20. "Off and Running: A Day at the Races"
21. winter term
22. Hindus
23. Oh my
24. O Lord
25. sociology courses

Exercise 2: Using Apostrophes to Show Possession
1. Mexico's
2. brother-in-law's
3. Joan's   Brothers'
4. Cameron, Rod, and Allison's
5. anyone's
6. Man's   men's
7. Mothers'
8. People's
9. Charles'
10. company's

Exercise 3: Using Apostrophes to Show Possession
1. Benny Wright's songs
2. Laurel and Hardy's films
3. the sun's rays
4. Nikki and Nikko's house
5. the sergeant-at-arms' power
6. the ladies' meeting
7. my sister-in-law's temper
8. the food servers' joy
9. the boys' temperament
10. the women's anger

Exercise 4: Using Apostrophes to Form Contractions and Plurals
1. They're   '98
2. whose
3. ten's
4. C
5. 8's   3's

Exercise 5: Using Abbreviations
1. Dr.
2. Thomas
3. feet
4. Ireland   nineteenth-century

5. mph or C
6. page chapter
7. C
8. population
9. dollars
10. Number
11. C
12. Monday
13. Southern California
14. Robert Psychology
15. Mr. Nevada
16. C
17. Harold and Maude
18. C
19. Ph.D
20. C

Exercise 6: Using Italics

1. Underline Crossfire, underline Newsweek
2. Underline Guernica, The Third of May, 1808
3. Underline The Primal Scream, Chattanooga Times, Interpretation of Dreams, c'est la vie
4. Circle Constitution
5. Circle Bible, Old Testament. Underline Absalom, Absalom and As I Lay Dying
6. Underline Bold Strokes: A Guide to Beautiful Handwriting, c's, o's, 7's 9's
7. C
8. Underline The Silver Streak
9. C
10. Underline Typhoon
11. Underline Rebel Without a Cause, Giant
12. Underline Raise the Titanic, The Dream of Eva Ryker

13. C
14. Underline hiss, pop, sizzle, buzz, hum
15. C
16. C
17. Underline smog, smoke, fog
18. C
19. Underline l's llama
20. Underline Oedipus Rex

Exercise 7: Using Hyphens

1. well-made thirty-five
2. anti-intellectualism
3. wall-less
4. one-fourth
5. president-elect
6. father- and mother-in-law
7. hard-nosed mean-eyed
8. little-known
9. re-creation
10. Out-of-state
11. C
12. Pre-World War I
13. forty-six well-developed fired-up
14. great-grandmother
15. hard-driving twenty-five
16. re-sign
17. hand-painted jack-in-the-box
18. self-confidence self-discipline
19. all-American
20. devil-take-the-hindmost I-told-you-so

Exercise 8: Using Numbers

1. Eighty-three 203
2. 102
3. ninety-five two hundred

4. 1865
5. C
6. four
7. 12 37
8. 2 42 7
9. 24 21
10. 9:00
11. 225
12. 3

13. five-thousand-acre 2010
14. 406 two thousand
15. seven twenty-two
16. first
17. 3,050 22,000
18. 8 1/2" x 11" 10" x 14"
19. C
20. ten-mile